What People Are Saying about *Threshold Bible Study*

"Besides furnishing the reader with solid biblical analysis, this remarkable series provides a method of study and reflection, for both individuals and groups, that is bound to produce rich fruit. This well-developed thematic approach to Bible study is meant to wed serious study and personal prayer within a reflective context. Stephen Binz is to be applauded for this fine addition to Bible study programs."

■ **DIANNE BERGANT, CSA**, professor of Old Testament, Catholic Theological Union, Chicago

"*Threshold Bible Study* connects the wisdom of God's Word to our daily lives. This fine series will provide needed tools that can deepen your understanding of Scripture, but most importantly it can deepen your faith. In the classical tradition of *lectio divina*, this series also offers a very practical way to pray with Scripture, and I can think of nothing better for equipping people for the New Evangelization than a biblically soaked life of prayer."

■ **MOST REVEREND CHARLES J. CHAPUT, OFM CAP.**, Archbishop of Denver

"Here, at last, is a Bible study for those of us who don't like Bible studies! Rather than focusing on a book, Stephen Binz invites us to view many well-known passages through the lens of a particular theme, bringing new meaning to the passages and deeper connection to the theme in our own lives. His discussions do far more than inform; they ask for commitment and assent on the part of the reader/prayer."

■ **KATHLEEN O'CONNELL CHESTO**, author of *F.I.R.E.* and *Why Are the Dandelions Weeds?*

"*Threshold Bible Study* offers a marvelous new approach for individuals and groups to study themes in our rich biblical and theological tradition. Moving through these thematic units feels like gazing at panels of stained glass windows, viewing similar images through different lights."

■ **JOHN ENDRES, SJ**, professor of Scripture, Jesuit School of Theology, Berkeley

"The Church has called Scripture a 'font' and 'wellspring' for the spiritual life. *Threshold Bible Study* is one of the best sources for tapping into the biblical font. Pope John Paul II has stressed that 'listening to the Word of God should become a life-giving encounter.' This is precisely what *Threshold Bible Study* offers to you—an encounter with the Word that will make your heart come alive."

■ **TIM GRAY**, Director of the Denver Catholic Biblical School

"*Threshold Bible Study* offers solid scholarship and spiritual depth. Drawing on the Church's living tradition and the Jewish roots of the New Testament, *Threshold Bible Study* can be counted on for lively individual study and prayer, even while it offers spiritual riches to deepen communal conversation and reflection among the people of God."

▨ **SCOTT HAHN**, Professor of biblical theology, Franciscan University of Steubenville

"Stephen Binz has extensive experience in developing materials for Bible study groups. He has taken the best features of *God's Word Today* magazine and adapted them for group use. *Threshold Bible Study* provides practical help in reading and sharing Scripture as God's word."

▨ **GEORGE MARTIN**, founding editor, *God's Word Today* magazine

"The distance many feel between the Word of God and their everyday lives can be overwhelming. It need not be so. *Threshold Bible Study* is a fine blend of the best of biblical scholarship and a realistic sensitivity to the spiritual journey of the believing Christian. I recommend it highly."

▨ **FRANCIS J. MOLONEY, SDB**, The Katharine Drexel Professor of Religious Studies, The Catholic University of America, Washington, DC

"I most strongly recommend Stephen Binz's *Threshold Bible Study* for adult Bible classes, religious education, and personal spiritual enrichment. The series is exceptional for its scholarly solidity, pastoral practicality, and clarity of presentation. The church owes Binz a great debt of gratitude for his generous and competent labor in the service of the Word of God."

▨ **PETER C. PHAN**, The Ignacio Ellacuría Professor of Catholic Social Thought, Georgetown University

"Written in a clear and concise style, *Threshold Bible Study* presents solid contemporary biblical scholarship, offers questions for reflection and/or discussion, and then demonstrates a way to pray from the Scriptures. All these elements work together to offer the reader a wonderful insight into how the sacred texts of our faith can touch our lives in a profound and practical way today. I heartily recommend this series to both individuals and to Bible study groups."

▨ **ABBOT GREGORY J. POLAN, OSB**, Conception Abbey and Seminary College

"*Threshold Bible Study* is that rare kind of program that will help one cross an elusive threshold—using the Bible effectively for prayer and spiritual enrichment. This user-friendly program will enhance any personal or group Bible study. Guaranteed to make your love of Scripture grow!"

▨ **RONALD D. WITHERUP, SS**, biblical scholar and author of *The Bible Companion*

THRESHOLD
BIBLE STUDY

ADVENT
LIGHT

Stephen J. Binz

**TWENTY-THIRD
PUBLICATIONS**
twentythirdpublications.com

Eighth printing 2018

TWENTY-THIRD PUBLICATIONS
One Montauk Avenue, Suite 200
New London, CT 06320
(860) 437-3012 or (800) 321-0411
www.twentythirdpublications.com

ISBN 978-1-58595-316-5
Library of Congress Catalog Card Number: 2006928081

Printed in the U.S.A.

Bayard   A division of Bayard, Inc.

Contents

LESSONS 13–18

LESSONS 19–24

LESSONS 25–30

How to Use
Threshold Bible Study

Each book in the *Threshold Bible Study* series is designed to lead you
through a new doorway of biblical awareness, to accompany you
across a unique threshold of understanding. The characters, places,
and images that you encounter in each of these topical studies will help you
explore fresh dimensions of your faith and discover richer insights for your
spiritual life.

Threshold Bible Study covers biblical themes in depth in a short amount
of time. Unlike more traditional Bible studies that treat a biblical book or
series of books, *Threshold Bible Study* aims to address specific topics within
the entire Bible. The goal is not for you to comprehend everything about each
passage, but rather for you to understand what a variety of passages from different books of the Bible reveals about the topic of each study.

Threshold Bible Study offers you an opportunity to explore the entire Bible
from the viewpoint of a variety of themes. The commentary that follows each
biblical passage launches your reflection about that passage and helps you
begin to see its significance within the context of your contemporary experience. The questions following the commentary challenge you to understand
the passage more fully and apply it to your own life. The prayer starter helps
conclude your study by integrating learning into your relationship with God.

These studies are designed for maximum flexibility. Each study is presented in a workbook format, with sections for reading, reflecting, writing,
discussing, and praying. Space for writing after each question is ideal for personal study and allows group members to prepare in advance for their discussion. The thirty lessons in each topic may be used by an individual over the
period of a month, or by a group for six sessions, with lessons to be studied
each week before the next group meeting. These studies are ideal for Bible
study groups, small Christian communities, adult faith formation, student
groups, Sunday school, neighborhood groups, and family reading, as well as
for individual learning.

The method of Threshold Bible Study is rooted in the classical tradition of *lectio divina*, an ancient yet contemporary means for reading the Scriptures reflectively and prayerfully. Reading and interpreting the text (*lectio*) is followed by reflective meditation on its message (*meditatio*). This reading and reflecting flows into prayer from the heart (*oratio* and *contemplatio*).

This ancient method assures us that Bible study is a matter of both the mind and the heart. It is not just an intellectual exercise to learn more and be able to discuss the Bible with others. It is, more importantly, a transforming experience. Reflecting on God's word, guided by the Holy Spirit, illumines the mind with wisdom and stirs the heart with zeal.

Following the personal Bible study, Threshold Bible Study offers a method for extending *lectio divina* into a weekly conversation with a small group. This communal experience will allow participants to enhance their appreciation of the message and build up a spiritual community (*collatio*). The end result will be to increase not only individual faith, but also faithful witness in the context of daily life (*operatio*).

Through the spiritual disciplines of Scripture reading, study, reflection, conversation, and prayer, you will experience God's grace more abundantly as your life is rooted more deeply in Christ. The risen Jesus said: "Listen! I am standing at the door, knocking; if you hear my voice and open the door, I will come in to you and eat with you, and you with me" (Rev 3:20). Listen to the Word of God, open the door, and cross the threshold to an unimaginable dwelling with God!

SUGGESTIONS FOR INDIVIDUAL STUDY

- Make your Bible reading a time of prayer. Ask for God's guidance as you read the Scriptures.

- Try to study daily, or as often as possible according to the circumstances of your life.

- Read the Bible passage carefully, trying to understand both its meaning and its personal application as you read. Some persons find it helpful to read the passage aloud.

- Read the passage in another Bible translation. Each version adds to your understanding of the original text.

- Allow the commentary to help you comprehend and apply the scriptural text. The commentary is only a beginning, not the last word on the meaning of the passage.

- After reflecting on each question, write out your responses. The very act of writing will help you clarify your thoughts, bring new insights, and amplify your understanding.

- As you reflect on your answers, think about how you can live God's word in the context of your daily life.

- Conclude each daily lesson by reading the prayer and continuing with your own prayer from the heart.

- Make sure your reflections and prayers are matters of both the mind and the heart. A true encounter with God's word is always a transforming experience.

- Choose a word or a phrase from the lesson to carry with you throughout the day as a reminder of your encounter with God's life-changing word.

- Share your learning experience with at least one other person whom you trust for additional insights and affirmation. The ideal way to share learning is in a small group that meets regularly.

SUGGESTIONS FOR GROUP STUDY

- Meet regularly; weekly is ideal. Try to be on time and make attendance a high priority for the sake of the group. The average group meets for about an hour.

- Open each session with a prepared prayer, a song, or a reflection. Find some appropriate way to bring the group from the workaday world into a sacred time of graced sharing.

- If you have not been together before, name tags are very helpful as a group begins to become acquainted with the other group members.

- Spend the first session getting acquainted with one another, reading the Introduction aloud, and discussing the questions that follow.

- Appoint a group facilitator to provide guidance to the discussion. The role of facilitator may rotate among members each week. The facilitator simply keeps the discussion on track; each person shares responsibility for the group. There is no need for the facilitator to be a trained teacher.

- Try to study the six lessons on your own during the week. When you have done your own reflection and written your own answers, you will be better prepared to discuss the six scriptural lessons with the group. If you have not had an opportunity to study the passages during the week, meet with the group anyway to share support and insights.

- Participate in the discussion as much as you are able, offering your thoughts, insights, feelings, and decisions. You learn by sharing with others the fruits of your study.

- Be careful not to dominate the discussion. It is important that everyone in the group be offered an equal opportunity to share the results of their work. Try to link what you say to the comments of others so that the group remains on the topic.

- When discussing your own personal thoughts or feelings, use "I" language. Be as personal and honest as is appropriate and be very cautious about giving advice to others.

- Listen attentively to the other members of the group so as to learn from their insights. The words of the Bible affect each person in a different way, so a group provides a wealth of understanding for each member.

- Don't fear silence. Silence in a group is as important as silence in personal study. It allows individuals time to listen to the voice of God's Spirit and the opportunity to form their thoughts before they speak.

- Solicit several responses for each question. The thoughts of different people will build on the answers of others and will lead to deeper insights for all.

- Don't fear controversy. Differences of opinion are a sign of a healthy and honest group. If you cannot resolve an issue, continue on, agreeing to disagree. There is probably some truth in each viewpoint.

- Discuss the questions that seem most important for the group. There is no need to cover all the questions in the group session.

- Realize that some questions about the Bible cannot be resolved, even by experts. Don't get stuck on some issue for which there are no clear answers.

- Whatever is said in the group is said in confidence and should be regarded as such.

- Pray as a group in whatever way feels comfortable. Pray for the members of your group throughout the week.

Schedule for Group Study

Session 1: Introduction   Date: _____

Session 2: Lessons 1–6   Date: _____

Session 3: Lessons 7–12   Date: _____

Session 4: Lessons 13–18   Date: _____

Session 5: Lessons 19–24   Date: _____

Session 6: Lessons 25–30   Date: _____

The people who walked in darkness have seen a great light; those who lived in a land of deep darkness—on them light has shined. ISA 9:2

Advent Light

Advent is a time for new understanding, for putting different pieces of God's revelation together so as to see the divine plan more clearly. We listen to the words of the ancient prophets, to the wisdom of Jesus, to the stories of his birth and infancy, and we make connections between them. Then we connect those truths to our own lives and our contemporary world and see ways God is acting anew, ways God continues to reveal the coming of Jesus to us today.

Our best model for this Advent search for understanding is Mary of Nazareth. Luke's text says of her, "Mary treasured all these words and pondered them in her heart" (Luke 2:19). What were these words that Mary treasured and pondered? They were the words of the ancient Scriptures that she had learned throughout her life, the words the angel had revealed to her, the words the shepherds said to her about her child, and the words that welled up within her as she sang her canticle of praise. By making connections between the ancient and the new, between her people Israel and her own life, Mary grew in understanding of God's plan and responded to God's will with her acceptance: "Let it be with me according to your word" (Luke 1:38).

Our task during the Advent season is to imitate Mary by pondering the word of God and allowing it to resonate within our hearts and pour into our lives. This study will put us in contact with the treasure of that word—the words of Israel's prophets, the words of the gospel writers, and the words of John the Baptist, Joseph, Mary, angels, and shepherds. Pondering these words will help us wait in watchful hope, to experience again the expectation and wonder they felt as they realized God was doing new things in the world and in their individual lives.

Advent is a time for us to understand that God is always doing something new. But it is also a time to realize that God has been doing new things for centuries and millennia. During this season, we return in our memories to our ancestors in faith, to those ancient Israelites who responded to God's initiative and became vessels of God's revelation in history. The fact that Jesus was born in the year 3760, according to the Jewish calendar, reminds us that God was working in human history long before the new era was established through the earthly life of his Son. The extensive history of our Israelite ancestors is our history of salvation, too. This is the season par excellence to recall that long history and make it our own.

Reflection and discussion

• What thoughts and feelings come to mind with the word "Advent"?

• What can Mary teach me about the Advent season?

Waiting with Expectancy and Joyful Hope

Advent is all about watching and waiting. It is an opportunity to focus on the attitude that is so essential to the Christian life—expectancy. This is a time to set our sights on the promise, reflect on the significance of that promise, and long for its realization. Our waiting is not a passive whiling the time away, but rather a time for standing on tiptoes with anticipation.

What is this promise for which we watch and wait? The word "advent" comes from the Latin *adventus*, which means "coming" or "arrival." It is the Advent of Christ, the coming of our Messiah, the arrival of the world's Savior. But hasn't Christ already come? Hasn't the promise of the Messiah's arrival already been fulfilled? Yes and no. Does the world look like it is experiencing its messianic age? Do our lives feel like our Savior has arrived? To the degree that we have not yet experienced the fullness of salvation that God wills for us, then Christ has not yet come fully into our world and into our lives.

Yes, the Messiah has come; salvation is offered to us; we trust in God's power to bring us the fullness for which we long. But we still live in Advent, watching and waiting. We know that Christ comes to us each day, through insights, people, and sacramental experiences. We know that Christ will meet each of us when our lives are complete in a much fuller way than we experience him in this life. We know that the world lives in hope because Christ will come again in glory to complete the work he has begun, the work of bringing all people and nations into the peace of God's kingdom.

So why set aside these four weeks to celebrate Advent, if Advent is really what our whole life—year-round—is about? Because in a historical period of time, the Messiah came into our world and left his mark. Though his coming was prophesied and anticipated for centuries, some recognized the Messiah when he came and others did not. Advent is the season for us to return to that time in which the Messiah first came into our world and to relive the anticipation of our ancestors. The Scriptures of Advent, which express the watchful waiting of our ancestors, form the model and inspiration for us as we continue to watch and wait for our Savior's coming. If we learn from the successes and the failures of our ancestors, maybe we will not be so neglectful of Christ's continued arrival in our lives and in our world.

Reflection and discussion

- What in my life have I anticipated with joyful hope? What can this experience tell me about waiting for Christ's coming?

- What is the difference between active and passive waiting? What are the implications for our spiritual lives?

Active Preparation

We often hear admonitions about the abuses of this season in our modern, consumerist society, about how we have turned Advent into a frenzied "To Do" list rather than a period of quiet hope. True, our December calendars often serve us more as a countdown of shopping days than as Advent calendars of holy anticipation. Yet, we do not have to be disparaging of the many events that mark this "most wonderful time of the year." The shopping and gift wrapping, decorating and baking, cards and parties, can all be expressions of the real "reason for the season." If our busy activities reflect the great activity of God in history and if our shopping and gift-giving reflect the great gift that God has given us, then everything we do this Advent can help us prepare and be watchful. It is not so much what we do, but how we do it and why we do it that is important this month. Awareness of our own hearts and reflection about our activities can be key ingredients to our becoming watchful people in this season of expectancy. Our exterior preparations must be matched by an interior preparation.

If the season of Advent had a patron saint, it would surely be John the Baptist. He was the last of that long line of prophets preparing God's people throughout history for the Messiah's coming. But he didn't prepare with a sweet sentimentality about a smiling baby born on a starry night. He proclaimed the message that those who were anticipating the Messiah must renew their own lives to get ready. "Reform your lives," he said, "God's reign is now at hand….Prepare the way of the Lord; straighten out the paths of his coming."

In ancient times, forerunners went ahead of a king who was making a journey. They would announce the king's coming and encourage the people to prepare themselves and their town for the royal arrival. John was this kind of herald for Jesus. He was the one who prepared the way for the Messiah.

This is the role of John the Baptist for us during the season of Advent. He helps us prepare our lives so that we will recognize the Messiah and give him a welcome that is appropriate for his royal presence. The real preparation to which John calls us is transformation of life. This Advent prophet tells us that our task is urgent, and halfway measures are not appropriate for Christ. "Bear fruits worthy of repentance" (Luke 3:8), he proclaims. Real conversion of our hearts must be evident in the way that we live. We should heed the call of the prophets and make this Advent a time of real change so that our royal Messiah will be welcomed into our lives.

Reflection and discussion

- How could the modern culture of December actually enhance rather than detract from the spirit of Advent for me?

- How could my exterior preparation and my interior preparation be more closely matched this year?

Anticipatory Light Before the Dawn

December is a season of light for many people. In ancient times, participants in the pagan Yule celebrations lit oil lamps during the dark winter when the days are shortest. Our spiritual ancestors in Judaism burned lamps during their Festival of Dedication, and today light the candles of the Hanukkah menorah, or Hanukiyah, as a sign of gratitude for God's saving presence. Christians light the candles of the Advent wreath as a symbol of increasing expectation. People of many religious persuasions light their homes and their cities during December.

Too often we call attention to what separates us from others; too seldom we highlight what joins us together. Christians often underline the fact that the Jewish people do not believe that the Messiah has come. Yet, during the season of Advent we can emphasize the fact that both Jews and Christians look forward with joyful hope to the Messiah's future coming. Both Jews and Christians look to the ancient prophets to understand the dawning light that God will bring in our future. Of course, the Jewish people hope for the Messiah's first manifestation, while Christians await his return in glory. But we can be sure that Jews and Christians together look forward to the future appearance of the same Messiah of God. The whole world awaits a time of peace and justice in the world; all people dream of a better future. And the God of all creation and all nations is the source of that trusting optimism. What better way to highlight our unity with the expectant people of our world than to celebrate Advent in a spirit of mutual hope.

The light of this season is light that brightens the darkness, the light that comes before the rising dawn. This is the anticipatory light that we will experience these weeks as we wait for Christmas. It is the light of ancient Israel's experience, the light of hope, as they awaited the dawning light of the Messiah.

With this flickering light of Advent, we can explore the darkness. By illuminating the shadows and reflecting on the gloom of our lives and our world, we can open our lives to watch and stand ready for what God is going to do next. Christ is the light of the world, the light for the nations, the light that will shine on those in darkness.

Christ has come and Christ will come again…and again, and again. We are people who wait in joyful hope. The Advent prayer of the early Church, "Come, Lord Jesus," is still answered in new and surprising ways.

Reflection and discussion

- In what way do the lights of this season help me cultivate a sense of expectation?

- What are my personal goals for Advent this year?

Prayer

God of all creation, you prepared a waiting world for the coming of your Son. Unite me this season with the ancient people of Israel who longed for the fulfillment of your covenant's promises and hoped for the advent of your kingdom. Give me a burning sense of anticipation, a joyful and optimistic spirit, and a fervent hope so that I can see the many ways in which you are manifesting yourself in our world. May I proclaim throughout Advent the zealous prayer of your community of disciples: "Come, Lord Jesus, come!"

SUGGESTIONS FOR FACILITATORS, GROUP SESSION 1

1. If the group is meeting for the first time, or if there are newcomers joining the group, it is helpful to provide nametags.

2. You may want to ask the participants to introduce themselves and tell a bit about themselves. Ask one or more of these introductory questions:
   - What drew you to join this group?
   - What is your biggest fear in beginning this Bible study?
   - How is beginning this study like a "threshold" for you?

3. Light a candle or oil lamp during this and future sessions to be kept burning throughout the discussion and prayer.

4. Distribute the books to the members of the group.

5. You may want to pray this prayer as a group:
   Come upon us, Holy Spirit, to enlighten and guide us as we begin this study of Advent Light. You inspired the scriptural writers throughout salvation history to anticipate the Messiah's coming into the world. Now penetrate our minds and our hearts to stir within us a spirit of longing for Christ. Motivate us to read the Scriptures, give us a love for God's word, and help us to look forward to the many ways you will manifest yourself throughout this study. Bless us during this session and throughout the coming week with the fire of your love.

6. Read the Introduction aloud, pausing at each question for discussion. Group members may wish to write the insights of the group as each question is discussed. Encourage several members to respond to each question.

7. Don't feel compelled to finish the complete Introduction during the session. It is better to allow sufficient time to talk about the questions raised than rush to the end. Group members may read any remaining sections on their own after the group meeting.

8. Instruct group members to read the first six lessons on their own during the days before the next group meeting. They should write out their own answers to the questions in preparation for next week's group discussion.

9. Fill in the date for each group meeting under "Schedule for Group Study."

10. Conclude by praying aloud together the prayer at the end of the Introduction.

"Have your lamps lit; be like those who are waiting for their master to return." LUKE 12:35–36

Burning with Anticipation

LUKE 12:35–48 ³⁵*"Be dressed for action and have your lamps lit;* ³⁶*be like those who are waiting for their master to return from the wedding banquet, so that they may open the door for him as soon as he comes and knocks.* ³⁷*Blessed are those slaves whom the master finds alert when he comes; truly I tell you, he will fasten his belt and have them sit down to eat, and he will come and serve them.* ³⁸*If he comes during the middle of the night, or near dawn, and finds them so, blessed are those slaves.*

³⁹*"But know this: if the owner of the house had known at what hour the thief was coming, he would not have let his house be broken into.* ⁴⁰*You also must be ready, for the Son of Man is coming at an unexpected hour."*

⁴¹*Peter said, "Lord, are you telling this parable for us or for everyone?"* ⁴²*And the Lord said, "Who then is the faithful and prudent manager whom his master will put in charge of his slaves, to give them their allowance of food at the proper time?* ⁴³*Blessed is that slave whom his master will find at work when he arrives.* ⁴⁴*Truly I tell you, he will put that one in charge of all his possessions.* ⁴⁵*But if that slave says to himself, 'My master is delayed in coming,' and if he begins to beat the other slaves, men and women, and to eat and drink and get drunk,* ⁴⁶*the master of that slave will come on a day when he does not expect him and at an hour that he does not know, and will cut him in pieces, and put him with the unfaithful.* ⁴⁷*That slave who knew what his master wanted, but did not prepare himself or do what*

was wanted, will receive a severe beating. [48]*But the one who did not know and did what deserved a beating will receive a light beating. From everyone to whom much has been given, much will be required; and from the one to whom much has been entrusted, even more will be demanded."*

N o attitude is more important for a Christian than that of watchful expectation. In parables and exhortations throughout the gospels, we see Jesus urging his followers to keep alert and to be ready for his coming. "Keep awake," he urges, "for you do not know on what day your Lord is coming" (Matt 24:42). "Keep alert, for you do not know when the time will come" (Mark 13:33). Don't sleep, stay awake, keep alert, be ready!

The lit lamps (verse 35) symbolize anticipation and preparedness. The oil lamps and, later, candles of the Christian tradition, remind us of the watchful hope in which we are called to live. Burning a candle while we read Scripture helps us focus on our reading and reminds us to be ready for the many ways Christ comes to us in God's word and in the daily experiences of life. Lighting candles in our homes and churches this season helps instill within us that necessary expectation of Christ's coming. Let's keep our lamps burning brightly around us and within our hearts.

The first parable concerns a master returning from a marriage feast. The servants are called "blessed" who remain awake and ready for his return (verse 37), even though he may return late into the night (verse 38). The second parable is about a homeowner and a thief. The homeowner must be prepared all the time because no one knows when a thief will come and disrupt his home (verse 39). The parables express the fact that Christ will return at a time we do not expect. So the only appropriate way to live is in continual and watchful readiness.

While the first part of the passage is addressed to all disciples (verses 35–40), the second part is particularly intended for Christian leaders (verses 41–48). The question of Peter (verse 41) makes the distinction between the Twelve and everyone else. Those in positions of leadership over others, whether they be parents, managers, pastors, catechists, or teachers, have particular responsibilities to always be alert and ready. Positions of leadership offer unusual temptations to the misuse of power and the abuse of those in their charge (verse 45). "The faithful and prudent manager" (verse 42) takes his responsibilities seriously and is always diligent with his duties, watchful for his master's return. He will be rewarded or punished according to the level of his knowledge and power (verses 46–48). The closing proverb is applicable to all who engage in active waiting for the Lord: "From everyone to whom much has been given, much will be required; and from the one to whom much has been entrusted, even more will be demanded" (verse 48).

Advent is the season in which we remind ourselves that watchfulness must pervade our entire lives. In the coming weeks we will look at the lives of God's people throughout biblical history so that we will learn better how to wait, to be ready, and to live in joyful hope.

Reflection and discussion

- Why is watchful anticipation so important for the Christian life?

- Do I live a drowsy life or one that is alert? What do I miss when my faith becomes lethargic?

- What do the lit lamps symbolize in Jesus' parable? How can oil lamps and candles be reminders for me?

- In what ways does Christ come unexpectedly into my life?

- What is the personal challenge offered me by the closing proverb of verse 48?

- Do I live in joyful hope? How could I expand my hope and deepen my joy?

Prayer

Come, Lord Jesus. Come with your Word, your presence, your gifts of grace. Help me not neglect the opportunities you give me to prepare myself for the fullness of your presence.

An account of the genealogy of Jesus the Messiah,
the son of David, the son of Abraham. MATT 1:1

The Messiah of Israel

MATTHEW 1:1–17 ¹*An account of the genealogy of Jesus the Messiah, the son of David, the son of Abraham.*

²*Abraham was the father of Isaac, and Isaac the father of Jacob, and Jacob the father of Judah and his brothers,* ³*and Judah the father of Perez and Zerah by Tamar, and Perez the father of Hezron, and Hezron the father of Aram,* ⁴*and Aram the father of Aminadab, and Aminadab the father of Nahshon, and Nahshon the father of Salmon,* ⁵*and Salmon the father of Boaz by Rahab, and Boaz the father of Obed by Ruth, and Obed the father of Jesse,* ⁶*and Jesse the father of King David.*

And David was the father of Solomon by the wife of Uriah, ⁷*and Solomon the father of Rehoboam, and Rehoboam the father of Abijah, and Abijah the father of Asaph,* ⁸*and Asaph the father of Jehoshaphat, and Jehoshaphat the father of Joram, and Joram the father of Uzziah,* ⁹*and Uzziah the father of Jotham, and Jotham the father of Ahaz, and Ahaz the father of Hezekiah,* ¹⁰*and Hezekiah the father of Manasseh, and Manasseh the father of Amos, and Amos the father of Josiah,* ¹¹*and Josiah the father of Jechoniah and his brothers, at the time of the deportation to Babylon.*

¹²*And after the deportation to Babylon: Jechoniah was the father of Salathiel, and Salathiel the father of Zerubbabel,* ¹³*and Zerubbabel the father of Abiud, and Abiud the father of Eliakim, and Eliakim the father of Azor,* ¹⁴*and Azor the father*

of Zadok, and Zadok the father of Achim, and Achim the father of Eliud, ¹⁵and Eliud the father of Eleazar, and Eleazar the father of Matthan, and Matthan the father of Jacob, ¹⁶and Jacob the father of Joseph the husband of Mary, of whom Jesus was born, who is called the Messiah.

¹⁷So all the generations from Abraham to David are fourteen generations; and from David to the deportation to Babylon, fourteen generations; and from the deportation to Babylon to the Messiah, fourteen generations.

I n the first few verses of the New Testament, Matthew links the coming of the Messiah with the ancient history of the people of Israel. Jesus is connected with the long list of names, going back to the earliest history of God's revelation to the Hebrew people. As the culmination of this long history, Jesus is shown to be the achievement of Israel's highest hopes, the one for whom that long history had prepared.

The first verse of the gospel introduces three names for Jesus that will be developed throughout the gospel. "Messiah" speaks of the anointed king who was expected to fulfill the longings for peace and the reign of God for which God's people yearned. "Son of David" is a messianic title proclaiming Jesus as a royal descendant from the line of King David. The title indicates that Jesus would complete the promises God made to David that his dynasty and his kingdom would endure forever (2 Sam 7:12, 16). "Son of Abraham" links Jesus with the beginnings of God's covenant with Israel, which he initiated with Abraham. The title indicates that Jesus would fulfill the promise that in the descendants of Abraham all the nations of the earth would gain blessing (Gen 22:18).

This genealogy writes the fathers and mothers of Israel into the family tree of Christians. Lest we think of this genealogy as merely a monotonous list of unpronounceable names, we are reminded very specifically that our identity in Christ is rooted in the memory of our ancestors in the Hebrew Scriptures. The history of Jesus did not begin in Nazareth or Bethlehem, for it contains the stories of ancient patriarchs, prophets, kings, and generations of men and women leading up to "Joseph the husband of Mary, of whom Jesus was born" (verse 16).

The word translated here as "genealogy" is the Greek word *genesis*, which can mean "birth," "beginning," "origin," or "genealogy" (verse 1). How we translate the word depends on whether the opening verse is an introduction to the genealogical list (for which it would be translated "genealogy") or to the first two chapters on the infancy of Jesus (for which it would be translated "birth") or to the whole gospel (for which it would be translated "origin" or "beginning"). It is quite possible that Matthew chose the word *genesis* in order to evoke associations with the first book of the Bible. In Jesus Christ, God was making a new beginning for both creation and humanity.

Reflection and discussion

- Why is it so important that the origins of Jesus be connected with both Abraham and David?

- Who are the people most responsible for bringing Christ to me? How did God use the life of each of these persons to draw closer to me?

Prayer

Son of Abraham and Son of David, the lives of individual people made the way ready for your coming to the world. May I live in such a way that I become an instrument of your coming and prepare the way in the life of another person.

Samuel took the horn of oil and anointed David in the presence of his brothers, and the spirit of the Lord came mightily upon David.

1 SAM 16:13

Anointed as Israel's Shepherd

1 SAMUEL 16:1–13 ¹*The Lord said to Samuel, "How long will you grieve over Saul? I have rejected him from being king over Israel. Fill your horn with oil and set out; I will send you to Jesse the Bethlehemite, for I have provided for myself a king among his sons." ²Samuel said, "How can I go? If Saul hears of it, he will kill me." And the Lord said, "Take a heifer with you, and say, 'I have come to sacrifice to the Lord.'" ³Invite Jesse to the sacrifice, and I will show you what you shall do; and you shall anoint for me the one whom I name to you." ⁴Samuel did what the Lord commanded, and came to Bethlehem. The elders of the city came to meet him trembling, and said, "Do you come peaceably?" ⁵He said, "Peaceably; I have come to sacrifice to the Lord; sanctify yourselves and come with me to the sacrifice." And he sanctified Jesse and his sons and invited them to the sacrifice.*

⁶When they came, he looked on Eliab and thought, "Surely the Lord's anointed is now before the Lord." ⁷But the Lord said to Samuel, "Do not look on his appearance or on the height of his stature, because I have rejected him; for the Lord does not see as mortals see; they look on the outward appearance, but the Lord looks on the heart." ⁸Then Jesse called Abinadab, and made him pass before Samuel. He said, "Neither has the Lord chosen this one." ⁹Then Jesse made Shammah pass by.

And he said, "Neither has the Lord chosen this one." ¹⁰Jesse made seven of his sons pass before Samuel, and Samuel said to Jesse, "The Lord has not chosen any of these." ¹¹Samuel said to Jesse, "Are all your sons here?" And he said, "There remains yet the youngest, but he is keeping the sheep." And Samuel said to Jesse, "Send and bring him; for we will not sit down until he comes here." ¹²He sent and brought him in. Now he was ruddy, and had beautiful eyes, and was handsome. The Lord said, "Rise and anoint him; for this is the one." ¹³Then Samuel took the horn of oil, and anointed him in the presence of his brothers; and the spirit of the Lord came mightily upon David from that day forward. Samuel then set out and went to Ramah.

I n order to recount the beginning of the reign of King David, the author takes us to the town of Bethlehem. Here we first encounter an unknown, unvalued shepherd boy tending his flock. The history recounted in the remainder of the book shows us how David rose to rule as the great "shepherd of Israel" because he was chosen and anointed by God.

God instructs the prophet Samuel to go to Jesse of Bethlehem, the father of eight sons (verse 1). God has chosen the new king from among Jesse's family. The mission is a hazardous one for Samuel, because the throne was not vacant; Saul was still the king. It is dangerous to anoint a king when a king already reigns. The elders of Bethlehem tremble at the coming of this kingmaker because of the political risk involved (verse 4). The sons of Jesse are paraded, one by one, before Samuel, but none of them proves to be the chosen one. God told Samuel not to be attracted by physical appearances, that what mattered to God is the heart. Instead of the most likely sons of Jesse, God had chosen the outsider, the least likely, the one without credentials—the one with the right heart (verse 7).

The action is halted; the elders, the prophet, Jesse and his sons, and the readers, too, wait in anticipation for the coming of David (verse 11). Finally David arrives. This is the one for whom Israel and even God himself has been watching in hopeful anticipation. God does a quick heart exam and declares, "This is the one" (verse 12). Samuel then anoints David with oil and establishes him as the future king.

The anointing oil identified and established David as the proper subject for the work of God's spirit. In choosing David, God began something new in the history of his people. Anointed with oil and with the spirit of God, David is sacramentally empowered by God to do his will, to be his instrument in moving toward God's vision of the kingdom. Though David continued to shepherd his flock and Samuel returned to Ramah (verse 13), the thrust of the narrative moves from Bethlehem to Jerusalem, where David will reign as king. Israel would never again be the same. David was now a man with an irreversible mission to establish the kingdom of God.

Reflection and discussion

- In what ways does God's choice of David prefigure that of Jesus?

- Are my standards for judging people similar to or different from those of God?

- What qualities of a shepherd are desirable in a king?

- How does God continue to choose the unlikely, those without credentials and social claims, today?

- What difference would it make if I saw people as God sees them? if I saw myself as God sees me?

- Why does God so often work in ways that are surprising, unexpected, and new?

Prayer

God of our ancestors, you have continually worked in unexpected, surprising ways throughout history. Do a new thing today in my life, and bless me beyond my routines and expectations with an outpouring of your grace.

**A shoot shall come out from the stock of Jesse,
and a branch shall grow out of his roots.** ISA 11:1

The Tree of Jesse Blooms

ISAIAH 10:33—11:10

³³*Look, the Sovereign, the Lord of hosts,*
　　will lop the boughs with terrifying power;
the tallest trees will be cut down,
　　and the lofty will be brought low.
³⁴*He will hack down the thickets of the forest with an axe,*
　　and Lebanon with its majestic trees will fall.

11 ¹*A shoot shall come out from the stock of Jesse,*
　　and a branch shall grow out of his roots.
²*The spirit of the Lord shall rest on him,*
　　the spirit of wisdom and understanding,
　　the spirit of counsel and might,
　　the spirit of knowledge and the fear of the Lord.
³*His delight shall be in the fear of the Lord.*
He shall not judge by what his eyes see,
　　or decide by what his ears hear;
⁴*but with righteousness he shall judge the poor,*
　　and decide with equity for the meek of the earth;
he shall strike the earth with the rod of his mouth,

and with the breath of his lips he shall kill the wicked.
⁵*Righteousness shall be the belt around his waist,*
   and faithfulness the belt around his loins.

⁶*The wolf shall live with the lamb,*
   the leopard shall lie down with the kid,
the calf and the lion and the fatling together,
   and a little child shall lead them.
⁷*The cow and the bear shall graze,*
   their young shall lie down together;
   and the lion shall eat straw like the ox.
⁸*The nursing child shall play over the hole of the asp,*
   and the weaned child shall put its hand on the adder's den.
⁹*They will not hurt or destroy*
   on all my holy mountain;
for the earth will be full of the knowledge of the Lord
   as the waters cover the sea.

¹⁰*On that day the root of Jesse shall stand as a signal to the peoples; the nations shall inquire of him, and his dwelling shall be glorious.*

This poetic text is one of the best-known prophetic passages about Israel's ideal future king, whom later Judaism and Christianity call the "Messiah." Isaiah proclaimed that a new anointed ruler would rise from the destruction of David's dynasty, a king filled with God's own spirit. His reign would be marked by an era of justice and peace, and all the nations would look to him.

The prophet begins by describing the kings in the line of King David under the image of a forest that has been chopped down (10:33–34). The once majestic trees have been decimated. But God remains true to his promises and gives new hope to his people by pledging that an ideal ruler would arise. From the hacked-off trunk and roots of Jesse, the father of David, a new shoot would grow (11:1). This future ruler would be anointed not only with oil, but with God's spirit—a spirit that would bestow upon him the character necessary to rule justly (11:2). These gifts of the spirit are qualities that belong to God alone, but are bestowed by God as gifts upon his chosen king. The future king would be far more righteous and faithful than King David or any of the other previous monarchs descended from David (11:3–5). He would render good judgments, speak the truth, and protect the rights of the poor.

The ideal king would establish an idyllic kingdom. The image of wild and dangerous animals existing together without threat or violence expresses the peace and harmony of the messianic age (11:6–8). War and destruction, so much a part of Israel's life through the centuries, will end, and the whole earth will know God (11:9). Isaiah envisions a planet in which everything is reversed from the evil and degradation of sin and shame. This is not a world turned upside down, but it is God's original intent for creation. It is the world turned right side up.

Isaiah looked to the future for fulfillment of hopes dashed in his own day. His prophecies were preserved after his death and directed toward another day, another Israel, another David. They gave voice to hopes for a new king, a new age, a new kingdom; they stood as a trusting anticipation of salvation to come.

Reflection and discussion

- Based on this passage from Isaiah, describe the meaning of the Advent symbol of the Jesse Tree.

- Describe the reign of Israel's ideal king as presented by Isaiah.

- Through baptism and confirmation, God has given me the gifts of the Spirit that were conferred on the Messiah. Which of the gifts of God's Spirit can I claim today to do God's work?

- In Isaiah's figurative portrait of the peaceful kingdom (verses 3–6), what types of people or situations could he have in mind?

- What can I do to promote God's peace for my little corner of the world?

Prayer

Jesus Christ, you are the flowering shoot on the family tree of Jesse. Let me claim your spiritual gifts: the gifts of wisdom, understanding, counsel, strength, knowledge, and reverence for God. May I use them for your glory and honor in what I say and do today.

**In the wilderness prepare the way of the Lord,
make straight in the desert a highway for our God.** ISA 40:3

Deliverance from Captivity

ISAIAH 40:1–11

¹*Comfort, O comfort my people,*
  says your God.
²*Speak tenderly to Jerusalem,*
  and cry to her
that she has served her term,
  that her penalty is paid,
that she has received from the Lord's hand
  double for all her sins.

³*A voice cries out:*
"In the wilderness prepare the way of the Lord,
  make straight in the desert a highway for our God.
⁴*Every valley shall be lifted up,*
  and every mountain and hill be made low;
the uneven ground shall become level,
  and the rough places a plain.
⁵*Then the glory of the Lord shall be revealed,*
  and all people shall see it together,
  for the mouth of the Lord has spoken."

⁶*A voice says, "Cry out!"*
   And I said, "What shall I cry?"
All people are grass,
   their constancy is like the flower of the field.
⁷*The grass withers, the flower fades,*
   when the breath of the Lord blows upon it;
   surely the people are grass.
⁸*The grass withers, the flower fades;*
   but the word of our God will stand for ever.
⁹*Get you up to a high mountain,*
   O Zion, herald of good tidings;
lift up your voice with strength,
   O Jerusalem, herald of good tidings,
   lift it up, do not fear;
say to the cities of Judah,
   "Here is your God!"
¹⁰*See, the Lord God comes with might,*
   and his arm rules for him;
his reward is with him,
   and his recompense before him.
¹¹*He will feed his flock like a shepherd;*
   he will gather the lambs in his arms,
   and carry them in his bosom,
   and gently lead the mother sheep.

This prophet of Israel's exile offers words of great hope, comfort, and consolation. In a period of tremendous adversity, God was turning again to his chosen people to bring them forgiveness and deliverance. God was coming to bring them out of their exile in Babylon and back to their own land, to the city of Jerusalem. From a period experienced as God's absence, God was creating an unmistakable experience of his divine presence.

The prophetic message is issued in a series of divine commands, the first of which is to "comfort my people, speak tenderly to Jerusalem" (verses 1–2). To a people mourning for their homeland and for the loss of God's presence,

God offers more than condolences and wishful thinking. God is removing the obstacles that have cut Israel off from its God. From the depths of God's steadfast commitment to the covenant relationship with his people, God is bringing deliverance and restored blessings through his people's repentance and divine forgiveness.

The second divine command is to "prepare the way of the Lord" (verse 3). God's gracious reentry into the life of his outcast people is described as a grand procession through the wilderness. God is always doing something new for his people. Just as God rescued the Israelites from Egypt in ancient days and brought them to their own land, so God would save Israel from their bondage in Babylon and return them to Jerusalem. The ultimate purpose for this great turn of events is so that God's presence will be manifested to all people: "The glory of the Lord shall be revealed, and all people shall see it together" (verse 5).

The third command is issued: "Cry out!" The announcement that all people are like the withering grass and the fading flower (verses 6–7) removes all distinctions in status and power. The one thing that matters is trust in the one promise that does not wither and fade, the one secure basis of hope and assurance: "The word of our God will stand forever" (verse 8).

The climactic announcement is reached as Jerusalem/Zion is called to proclaim God's imminent coming: "Here is your God!" (verse 9). God's advent is elaborated with two images: God comes as the mighty and victorious warrior to deliver his people (verse 10), and he comes as the gentle shepherd offering tender protection to each of his sheep (verse 11).

The prophet speaks God's word for every age. All of the gospels describe John the Baptist as the voice that cries out, "Prepare the way of the Lord." In our day too the glory of the Lord will be revealed and he will come to save his people.

Reflection and discussion

- What good news have I received? Did I prepare for that good news, or did it come suddenly?

- In what practical way have I experienced the truth of verse 8?

- Describe the two contrasting images of God in verses 10 and 11. Why are both images important for me?

- Which words of this prophet could give me the most hope in difficult times?

Prayer

God of our ancestors, you give me words of comfort and hope in your word which stands forever. Help me believe that you will bring renewal to my life and trust in your promises.

For you who revere my name the sun of righteousness shall rise, with healing in its wings. MAL 4:2

Healing Rays and Joyful Light

MALACHI 2:17—3:7; 4:1–6 ¹⁷*You have wearied the Lord with your words. Yet you say, "How have we wearied him?" By saying, "All who do evil are good in the sight of the Lord, and he delights in them." Or by asking, "Where is the God of justice?"*

3 ¹*See, I am sending my messenger to prepare the way before me, and the Lord whom you seek will suddenly come to his temple. The messenger of the covenant in whom you delight—indeed, he is coming, says the Lord of hosts. ²But who can endure the day of his coming, and who can stand when he appears?*

For he is like a refiner's fire and like fullers' soap; ³he will sit as a refiner and purifier of silver, and he will purify the descendants of Levi and refine them like gold and silver, until they present offerings to the Lord in righteousness. ⁴Then the offering of Judah and Jerusalem will be pleasing to the Lord as in the days of old and as in former years.

⁵Then I will draw near to you for judgment; I will be swift to bear witness against the sorcerers, against the adulterers, against those who swear falsely, against those who oppress the hired workers in their wages, the widow, and the orphan, against those who thrust aside the alien, and do not fear me, says the Lord of hosts.

⁶*For I the Lord do not change; therefore you, O children of Jacob, have not per-ished. ⁷Ever since the days of your ancestors you have turned aside from my statutes and have not kept them. Return to me, and I will return to you, says the Lord of hosts. But you say, "How shall we return?"*

4 ¹*See, the day is coming, burning like an oven, when all the arrogant and all evil-doers will be stubble; the day that comes shall burn them up, says the Lord of hosts, so that it will leave them neither root nor branch. ²But for you who revere my name the sun of righteousness shall rise, with healing in its wings. You shall go out leap-ing like calves from the stall. ³And you shall tread down the wicked, for they will be ashes under the soles of your feet, on the day when I act, says the Lord of hosts.*

⁴*Remember the teaching of my servant Moses, the statutes and ordinances that I commanded him at Horeb for all Israel.*

⁵*Lo, I will send you the prophet Elijah before the great and terrible day of the Lord comes. ⁶He will turn the hearts of parents to their children and the hearts of children to their parents, so that I will not come and strike the land with a curse.*

These final verses of the Old Testament end on a note of anticipa-tion. The "sun of justice" will rise (4:2). All that God has been doing throughout salvation history has been preparing for the new dawn that the God of justice (2:17) will bring. Despite the people's disregard for God's will in their lives and their injustices (3:5), God "does not change" (3:6). He remains the God of covenant love, pressing forward to fulfill his loving purposes and to establish his just order for the world. Thus, he comes to his people not as a consuming fire but as a refining flame (3:2–4), seek-ing to create from his people pure silver and gold without a speck of dross. Through the words of Malachi, God calls the people to "return" after turning aside from God's covenant: "Return to me and I will return to you, says the Lord of hosts" (3:7).

The day of the Lord's coming will bring both the fire of destruction and the rays of healing, depending on the disposition of those on whom the light of the "sun of justice" falls. The light will reduce the faithless to stubble, burn-ing away branches and even roots. But that same sun will bring a healing warmth and a joyful light to those who have returned and revere God (4:1–

3). God does not give up on his people, and helps them prepare for the day of his coming so that more will be saved.

The Lord's coming will be preceded by the "messenger," the one who will "prepare the way" (3:1). The messenger's identity is not given until the end of the book, when he is identified with the prophet Elijah (4:5). Like Elijah of old who converted the hearts of God's people, the new Elijah will turn the hearts of many to trust in the God of the covenant. The New Testament sees the fulfillment of this passage in the appearance of John the Baptist as the messenger and Jesus Christ as the Lord who is coming. Jesus taught that John is the messenger foretold in Malachi, saying of him, "If you are willing to accept it, he is Elijah who is to come" (Matt 11:10, 14).

The last book of the Old Testament, like the last book of the New Testament, urges readiness for the Lord's coming: "See, the day is coming" (4:1); "See I am coming soon" (Rev 22:7). Malachi, like the book of Revelation, issues a final warning as well as a call to repentance and conversion. God's reign has broken into history in the person of Jesus Christ. He is the Lord of justice.

Reflection and discussion

- The people ask Malachi, "How shall we return?" (3:7) In what ways is this prophet challenging me to return to God during this season?

- When are the rays of God's light a consuming fire of destruction and when are they a refining and healing light?

- What indications do I have that God has put me through the refiner's fire and refused to give up on me?

- What is comforting and reassuring for me in the prophet's words, "The Lord does not change" (3:6)?

- In what way does Israel's ancient prophets help me to be ready for Christ's coming?

Prayer

Sun of justice, your healing and revitalizing rays shine into our world seeking to bring us life and growth. Help me to return to you, so that my life will be prepared for the dawn of your coming.

SUGGESTIONS FOR FACILITATORS, GROUP SESSION 2

1. If there are newcomers who were not present for the first group session, introduce them now.

2. You may want to light a candle and pray this prayer as a group:
   Lord of Light, you urge your people to stay awake, to be ready, to wait in joyful hope. You have called us to be children of the light and to keep the flame of faith alive in our hearts until you come in glory. Throughout history, you have counseled your people to trust not in the passing things of this world, but in the word of God which stands forever. Gather us around your word, allow it to penetrate our hearts, and help us put it into practice in our daily lives. Bless us with your Holy Spirit as we learn together to live with burning anticipation.

3. Ask one or more of the following questions:
   - What was your biggest challenge in Bible study over this past week?
   - What did you learn about yourself as a disciple this week?

4. Discuss lessons 1 through 6 together. Assuming that group members have read the Scripture and commentary during the week, there is no need to read it aloud. As you review each lesson, you might want to briefly summarize the Scripture passage of each lesson and ask the group what stands out most clearly about the commentary.

5. Choose one or more of the questions for reflection and discussion from each lesson to talk over as a group. You may want to ask group members which question was most challenging or helpful to them as you review each lesson.

6. Keep the discussion moving, but don't rush the discussion in order to complete more questions. Allow time for the questions that provoke the most discussion.

7. Remember that there are no definitive answers for these discussion questions. The insights of group members will add to the understanding of all. None of these questions requires an expert.

8. Instruct group members to complete lessons 7 through 12 on their own during the six days before the next group meeting. They should write out their own answers to the questions as preparation for next week's session.

9. Conclude by praying aloud together the prayer at the end of lesson 6, or any other prayer you choose.

With the spirit and power of Elijah he will go before the Lord, to make ready a people prepared for the Lord. LUKE 1:17

Preparing a People for the Lord

LUKE 1:5–25 *⁵In the days of King Herod of Judea, there was a priest named Zechariah, who belonged to the priestly order of Abijah. His wife was a descendant of Aaron, and her name was Elizabeth. ⁶Both of them were righteous before God, living blamelessly according to all the commandments and regulations of the Lord. ⁷But they had no children, because Elizabeth was barren, and both were getting on in years.*

⁸Once when he was serving as priest before God and his section was on duty, ⁹he was chosen by lot, according to the custom of the priesthood, to enter the sanctuary of the Lord and offer incense. ¹⁰Now at the time of the incense-offering, the whole assembly of the people was praying outside. ¹¹Then there appeared to him an angel of the Lord, standing at the right side of the altar of incense. ¹²When Zechariah saw him, he was terrified; and fear overwhelmed him. ¹³But the angel said to him, "Do not be afraid, Zechariah, for your prayer has been heard. Your wife Elizabeth will bear you a son, and you will name him John. ¹⁴You will have joy and gladness, and many will rejoice at his birth, ¹⁵for he will be great in the sight of the Lord. He must never drink wine or strong drink; even before his birth he will be filled with the Holy Spirit. ¹⁶He will turn many of the people of Israel to the Lord their God. ¹⁷With the spirit and power of Elijah he will go before him, to turn the hearts of *parents to their children, and the disobedient to the wisdom of the righteous, to make ready a people prepared for the Lord." *[18]*Zechariah said to the angel, "How will I know that this is so? For I am an old man, and my wife is getting on in years." *[19]*The angel replied, "I am Gabriel. I stand in the presence of God, and I have been sent to speak to you and to bring you this good news. *[20]*But now, because you did not believe my words, which will be fulfilled in their time, you will become mute, unable to speak, until the day these things occur."*

*[21]*Meanwhile, the people were waiting for Zechariah, and wondered at his delay in the sanctuary. *[22]*When he did come out, he could not speak to them, and they realized that he had seen a vision in the sanctuary. He kept motioning to them and remained unable to speak. *[23]*When his time of service was ended, he went to his home.*

*[24]*After those days his wife Elizabeth conceived, and for five months she remained in seclusion. She said, *[25]*"This is what the Lord has done for me when he looked favorably on me and took away the disgrace I have endured among my people."*

A mood of expectation fills the opening chapters of Luke's gospel. The characters that populate its verses represent the faithful people of God who are waiting for the dawn of salvation. The account begins with the coming of John the Baptist. While the other gospels describe John's public ministry, only Luke begins with his parents and his infancy.

Zechariah was a priest; Elizabeth was from the priestly family of Aaron. Both personify Jewish devotion at its best. Their faithful adherence to their ancient religion enabled them to perceive the new era of salvation initiated by the God of their ancestors. In the Jewish culture of the time, their advanced age and childlessness represented a condition of hopelessness. But the message of the angel to Zechariah and the pregnancy of Elizabeth shows how God reverses human expectations; the humanly impossible become divinely possible for those who trust in God.

The long history of divine promises and human longing is spiraling into Judea. The elderly and childless state of Zechariah and Elizabeth recall the condition of the first parents of Israel, Abraham and Sarah. Through these ancient ancestors God promised that "all the families of the earth shall be blessed" (Gen 12:3). That ancient covenant is recalled as God remembers his promises and ushers in the final covenant of grace.

The waiting of Zechariah before he could speak again and the waiting of the people outside the temple during Zechariah's delay (verses 20–21) reflects the wait of God's people for the promised "joy and gladness" (verse 14). Within the narrative the wait creates a mood of anticipation for what would happen next. It is the watchful expectation of Advent, waiting for God's next move. *moments of visitation sensitivity*

The child Zechariah and Elizabeth wanted was the man God wanted; what God gave to that couple he also gave to the world. In describing John's role, the angel proclaims that he would "make ready a people prepared for the Lord," and that he would go forth "with the spirit and power of Elijah" (verse 17). His role in salvation was to "turn many of the people of Israel to the Lord, their God" (verse 16) so that they would be ready for the new day of salvation God was bringing upon the world.

Reflection and discussion

- What conditions in my life would be considered hopeless were it not for God? *Preparing for death own or loved one*

- In what ways are Zechariah and Elizabeth like Abraham and Sarah? *old barren gave up hope for a child*

- For what in my life have I had to wait? What good can be found in waiting?

  trust
  patience &
  answer to prayer

- Who are models of trust for me? How has their trust allowed God to work?

  — M. Bourgeous
  Gorini
  Fr. Ken — led by H. Spirit

- How can I cultivate an outlook of expectancy?

  sensitive
  responsive to moments
  of visitation
  to God's touch

Prayer

God of all hope, teach me how to wait in joyful hope for the fulfillment of your promises. Fill my life with a spirit of trust so that I will be confident in your saving love for me.

You will conceive in your womb and bear a son, and you will name him Jesus. LUKE 1:31

Conceived of the Holy Spirit

LUKE 1:26–38 ²⁶*In the sixth month the angel Gabriel was sent by God to a town in Galilee called Nazareth, ²⁷to a virgin engaged to a man whose name was Joseph, of the house of David. The virgin's name was Mary. ²⁸And he came to her and said, "Greetings, favored one! The Lord is with you." ²⁹But she was much perplexed by his words and pondered what sort of greeting this might be. ³⁰The angel said to her, "Do not be afraid, Mary, for you have found favor with God. ³¹And now, you will conceive in your womb and bear a son, and you will name him Jesus. ³²He will be great, and will be called the Son of the Most High, and the Lord God will give to him the throne of his ancestor David. ³³He will reign over the house of Jacob for ever, and of his kingdom there will be no end." ³⁴Mary said to the angel, "How can this be, since I am a virgin?" ³⁵The angel said to her, "The Holy Spirit will come upon you, and the power of the Most High will overshadow you; therefore the child to be born will be holy; he will be called Son of God. ³⁶And now, your relative Elizabeth in her old age has also conceived a son; and this is the sixth month for her who was said to be barren. ³⁷For nothing will be impossible with God." ³⁸Then Mary said, "Here am I, the servant of the Lord; let it be with me according to your word." Then the angel departed from her.*

The announcement of the angel to Mary signaled that the long-awaited time of the Messiah's coming was at hand. Centuries of watchful yearning were culminating in the conception of Israel's Messiah in the womb of Mary. Though the young woman had no idea what being the mother of Israel's Messiah would mean for her, she gave herself wholeheartedly to the call: "Let it be with me according to your word" (verse 38).

While the angelic birth announcement to Zechariah and Elizabeth had followed the pattern of many miraculous conceptions to elderly couples in the Old Testament, God's intervention in the life of Mary was unlike anything ever before in salvation history. The insistence that Mary was a virgin (verse 27) highlights the radical newness of God's action. God's intervention was not in response to her yearning for a child, nor was it the result of anything she could have anticipated. God was doing an extraordinarily new thing in response to the watchful longing of his people.

The heart of the annunciation scene declares the identity of the child to be born. He would be the Messiah, the one who would be given the throne of King David with an unending kingdom (verses 32–33), and he would be the Son of God, because he would be conceived through the overshadowing power of God's Holy Spirit (verse 35). The Church's earliest theology, reflected in Paul's writings, expresses this dual nature of Mary's child: "descended from David according to the flesh and declared to be son of God according to the spirit" (Rom 1:3–4).

He would be a divine king. Unlike King David, whose reign was bounded by time and space, this king would fulfill all of history and embrace all of time, and "of his kingdom there will be no end" (verse 33). But he would come not in terrible glory, blinding light, or trumpet blast. He would come through Mary's womb, a hungry and crying child, the hope of all the world.

Mary is the model of Advent because she was a woman of God's word. She received the word of God in her heart and consented to conceive the Son of God in her womb. Through the severe contractions of her uterus, eternity would enter time. She would be the threshold of the Lord into our world. During this season, may the Lord enter us spiritually as he entered Mary bodily, and may he daily enter the world through us as once he was born from her.

Reflection and discussion

- How was the response of Mary different from that of Zechariah (verses 18, 38)? Why was Mary able to trust God so completely?

  Z — doubt
  m — open-gave herself whole heartedly

- What does the annunciation passage teach us about the identity of Jesus?

  dual nature
  descended from David
  according to flesh
  son of God according to Spirit

- In what areas of life do I need to hear the words of the angel: "Do not be afraid," and "nothing is impossible with God?"

  facing death

  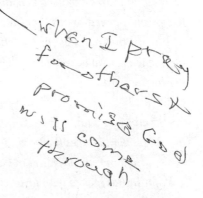
  when I pray for others & promised God will come through

Prayer

Most High God, you responded to the watchful longing of a waiting world. Teach me to respond to you like Mary, most blessed among women. Let your will be done in me according to your word.

"My soul magnifies the Lord, and my spirit rejoices in God my Savior."
LUKE 1:46–47

Pregnant with Child and with Hope

LUKE 1:39–56 ³⁹*In those days Mary set out and went with haste to a Judean town in the hill country,* ⁴⁰*where she entered the house of Zechariah and greeted Elizabeth.* ⁴¹*When Elizabeth heard Mary's greeting, the child leapt in her womb. And Elizabeth was filled with the Holy Spirit* ⁴²*and exclaimed with a loud cry, "Blessed are you among women, and blessed is the fruit of your womb.* ⁴³*And why has this happened to me, that the mother of my Lord comes to me?* ⁴⁴*For as soon as I heard the sound of your greeting, the child in my womb leapt for joy.* ⁴⁵*And blessed is she who believed that there would be a fulfillment of what was spoken to her by the Lord."*

⁴⁶*And Mary said,*
"My soul magnifies the Lord,
    ⁴⁷*and my spirit rejoices in God my Savior,*
⁴⁸*for he has looked with favor on the lowliness of his servant.*
    Surely, from now on all generations will call me blessed;
⁴⁹*for the Mighty One has done great things for me,*
    and holy is his name.

⁵⁰His mercy is for those who fear him
   from generation to generation.
⁵¹He has shown strength with his arm;
   he has scattered the proud in the thoughts of their hearts.
⁵²He has brought down the powerful from their thrones,
   and lifted up the lowly;
⁵³he has filled the hungry with good things,
   and sent the rich away empty.
⁵⁴He has helped his servant Israel,
   in remembrance of his mercy,
⁵⁵according to the promise he made to our ancestors,
   to Abraham and to his descendants for ever."
   ⁵⁶And Mary remained with her for about three months and then returned
to her home.

Perhaps the best analogy for the waiting of Advent is the experience of pregnancy. A mother-to-be waits for movements and the stirrings of new life. It is a time of expectant longing and joyful anticipation. In these verses, two pregnant women fill the scene. One is elderly and will have a son who will be the last great figure of ancient Israel; the other is young and will have a son who will usher in the new age of salvation. Their visit represents the meeting of the old covenant and the new, a completion and a new beginning of God's saving work.

Elizabeth proclaimed of Mary, "Blessed are you among women, and blessed is the fruit of your womb" (verse 42). God has exalted Mary among all the women of Israel: Sarah, Rachel, Miriam, Hannah, Deborah, and Judith; for God has chosen Mary to bring forth the hope of all the ages. Elizabeth called Mary "the mother of my Lord" (verse 43), the most exalted role of anyone in God's saving plan for the world. Yet, Mary is "blessed" not just because she is chosen by God to be mother of the Messiah, but because she is a woman of God's word: "blessed is she who believed that there would be a fulfillment of what was spoken to her by the Lord" (verse 45; see Luke 8:21; 11:28). Because of God's grace at work within Mary, all future generations will call her "blessed" (verse 48).

Deep within Elizabeth's womb, John leapt for joy as he recognized the presence of his redeemer in Mary's womb (verses 41, 44). Already filled with the Holy Spirit, already preparing the way, the tiny prophet expressed his first prophecy. John was beginning his lifelong mission of proclaiming the Messiah's coming.

Mary blossomed like a rose and her whole being unfolded with praise and thankfulness to God. In her canticle, Mary praised God for all the favors he had done for her and for everyone in every age; for reversing the world's expectations; and for exalting the lowly and needy. She placed herself within the long line of promises God made to Abraham and his descendants. She was humble enough to experience joy and gratitude for what God was doing through her.

Reflection and discussion

- What have been my most significant experiences of expectation and anticipation?

- In what ways is Advent like the experience of pregnancy?

- Why is Mary honored in Luke's gospel? Why will all future generations call her "blessed"?

a woman of God's word because of God's grace at work within her

- In what way does John's leaping in his mother's womb foretell his future mission?

  recognized presence of Jesus - his redeemer filled with H. Sp already preparing the way beginning his life long mission

- What would I include in my canticle of praise for God's blessings?

  gift

- What can I learn from Mary about Advent?

Prayer

God my Savior, you have looked upon me with favor and you continually reverse my expectations. Show me your power, your holiness, and your mercy, which you have shown in every age.

**By the tender mercy of our God,
the dawn from on high will break upon us.** LUKE 1:78

Breaking Dawn
Illumines the Darkness

LUKE 1:57–80 ⁵⁷*Now the time came for Elizabeth to give birth, and she bore a son.* ⁵⁸*Her neighbors and relatives heard that the Lord had shown his great mercy to her, and they rejoiced with her.*

⁵⁹*On the eighth day they came to circumcise the child, and they were going to name him Zechariah after his father.* ⁶⁰*But his mother said, "No; he is to be called John."* ⁶¹*They said to her, "None of your relatives has this name."* ⁶²*Then they began motioning to his father to find out what name he wanted to give him.* ⁶³*He asked for a writing-tablet and wrote, "His name is John." And all of them were amazed.* ⁶⁴*Immediately his mouth was opened and his tongue freed, and he began to speak, praising God.* ⁶⁵*Fear came over all their neighbors, and all these things were talked about throughout the entire hill country of Judea.* ⁶⁶*All who heard them pondered them and said, "What then will this child become?" For, indeed, the hand of the Lord was with him.*

⁶⁷*Then his father Zechariah was filled with the Holy Spirit and spoke this prophecy:*
⁶⁸*"Blessed be the Lord God of Israel,*
   for he has looked favorably on his people and redeemed them.

⁶⁹*He has raised up a mighty savior for us*
   in the house of his servant David,
⁷⁰*as he spoke through the mouth of his holy prophets from of old,*
   ⁷¹*that we would be saved from our enemies*
      and from the hand of all who hate us.
⁷²*Thus he has shown the mercy promised to our ancestors,*
   and has remembered his holy covenant,
⁷³*the oath that he swore to our ancestor Abraham,*
   to grant us ⁷⁴*that we, being rescued from the hands of our enemies,*
might serve him without fear, ⁷⁵*in holiness and righteousness*
   before him all our days.
⁷⁶*And you, child, will be called the prophet of the Most High;*
   for you will go before the Lord to prepare his ways,
⁷⁷*to give knowledge of salvation to his people*
   by the forgiveness of their sins.
⁷⁸*By the tender mercy of our God,*
   the dawn from on high will break upon us,
⁷⁹*to give light to those who sit in darkness and in the shadow of death,*
   to guide our feet into the way of peace."
⁸⁰*The child grew and became strong in spirit, and he was in the wilderness until*
the day he appeared publicly to Israel.

Zechariah's long wait ended when he wrote, "His name is John" (verse 63). Immediately he could speak again and praise God. The name John means "Yahweh has shown favor," expressing John's origin and his future. A sense of anticipation rippled across the countryside of Judea as the people asked with amazement and fear, "What then will this child become?" (verse 66). The answer is hinted at in the canticle of Zechariah, but the more complete reply unfolds in the later ministry of John the Baptist. Zechariah's canticle describes the advent of salvation in the language and imagery of the Old Testament. The hopes of Israel would be fulfilled as God kept his promises to David and his oath to Abraham. The covenant established through Abraham, Moses, and David would be the foundation of God's merciful relationship with Israel and the root of all God's promises.

I will be your God
you will be my people

Jesus would be called "Son of the Most High" (verse 32); John would be called "prophet of the Most High" (verse 76). "You will go before the Lord to prepare his ways" describes John's preparatory role. He was to unveil the "knowledge of salvation" by the forgiveness of sins (verse 77). By giving people a foretaste, John would prepare them to accept the full salvation and forgiveness that God wishes for all.

The coming of Christ is called the "dawn from on high" (verse 78). This daybreak that illuminates the night is a term used by Jews to describe the expected Messiah (see Mal 4:2; Isa 60:1–2). This rising light would illuminate the Lord's way that John would prepare; it would shine on those in darkness and brighten the way that leads to peace (verse 79).

The mercy of God is that astonishing gift we thought impossible to receive, the marvel we thought we were too old to receive (verse 58). "The mercy promised to our ancestors" (verse 72) was manifested in the Savior's coming "by the tender mercy of our God" (verse 78). That mercy comes like a baby, a completely new gift, but one we must protect and nurture it. When faith arises from the depths of our hopelessness; when we suddenly find forgiveness in a heart filled with resentment; when we discover confidence when fear was about to consume us: this is divine mercy. Whenever the impossible gift arrives for us, a gift we have neither earned nor deserved, we can do nothing less than rejoice (verse 58).

Reflection and discussion

- In what way is the Canticle of Zechariah (verses 68–79) both similar to and different from the Canticle of Mary (verses 46–55)?

× Zech O.T.
– Mary N.T.

- How did the neighbors of Zechariah and Elizabeth respond to these events (verses 58, 65–66)?

  rejoiced Fear pondering

- When have I experienced divine mercy?

  after Resurrection J. treated apostles as though nothing had happened

- Of the promises listed in Zechariah's Canticle, which one resonates most clearly with me?

  shown his mercy

- What can I learn from Elizabeth and Zechariah about Advent?

  *trust be faithful * nothing impossible * God can use us at any age*

Prayer

Lord God of Israel, you have shown your mercy, remembered your covenant, and brought to us a Savior. Illumine my darkness, dispel my shadows, and guide me in your ways with your shining light.

"The one who is more powerful than I is coming after me."

MARK 1:7

A Prophet's Voice
in the Wilderness

MARK 1:1–8 ¹*The beginning of the good news of Jesus Christ, the Son of God.*
   ²*As it is written in the prophet Isaiah,*
   "See, I am sending my messenger ahead of you,
      who will prepare your way;
   ³*the voice of one crying out in the wilderness:*
      'Prepare the way of the Lord,
      make his paths straight,'"
⁴*John the baptizer appeared in the wilderness, proclaiming a baptism of repentance for the forgiveness of sins.* ⁵*And people from the whole Judean countryside and all the people of Jerusalem were going out to him, and were baptized by him in the river Jordan, confessing their sins.* ⁶*Now John was clothed with camel's hair, with a leather belt around his waist, and he ate locusts and wild honey.* ⁷*He proclaimed, "The one who is more powerful than I is coming after me; I am not worthy to stoop down and untie the thong of his sandals.* ⁸*I have baptized you with water; but he will baptize you with the Holy Spirit."*

While the gospels of Matthew and Luke prepare for the coming of Jesus by recounting his conception and birth, the gospel of Mark sets the stage for Jesus by describing the adult ministry of John the Baptist. His role was to stir up the people, challenge them to look carefully at their lives, and prepare their hearts for Christ. John was evidently saying something that people needed to hear; the whole countryside and all Jerusalem came to listen to him (verse 5).

The prophetic words that introduce the passage create a mood of expectancy (verses 2–3). The words are formed from Exodus 23:20, in which God promises to send an angelic messenger ahead of his people in the wilderness to lead them to freedom, and from the promising words of Malachi 3:1 and Isaiah 40:3. The people of Israel were looking forward to a revival of prophecy, and John seemed to cause great excitement with his message. He dressed the part of the prophet (verse 6; see 2 Kings 1:8); indeed he seemed to be Elijah returned (Mark 9:11–13). His message was that of repentance, the call to turn around, to change one's heart, will, and actions.

Advent leads us into the wilderness to confront the message of John the Baptist. He's not an easy person to fit into this festive season. There are no Christmas carols about John the Baptist and he's not the kind of guest we would invite to a holiday party. His message of repentance is not the kind of thing quoted in greeting cards. But he is the Advent patron, the one who prepares the way and sets lives straight for the Savior's coming. Confronting this prophet is more about sand in our face and thirst in our throat.

John's message was spoken to men and women of ancient Judah, but like the words of all the prophets, his words are also meant for us today. We need to hear John's sober call to repentance in the emptiness of our own wilderness. We need to hear the message of forgiveness, and to know that we can draw near to God. We can make our hearts ready for Jesus by turning away from all that could separate us from him. "Repent," cries the prophet. Change your old ways. Get out of your rut. The way to Bethlehem leads through the desert of Judea.

Reflection and discussion

- What was so attractive about this harsh prophet in the wilderness?

*caused great excitement
with his message
stir up the people
create atmosphere
of expectancy*

- Why does the gospel describe the clothing and diet of John? Why is the wilderness an important context for Advent?

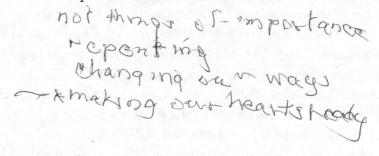

*not things of importance
repenting
changing our ways
→ making our hearts ready*

- Who has been a John the Baptist for me—someone who challenged me to change my heart, who set me straight or prepared me for something new?

*Retreat director—
Joe Currie
Ken
Fred Maples*

Prayer

Coming One, prepare my life with repentance to welcome and receive you.
May I be a herald of your coming into the lives of those around me.

"I came baptizing with water for this reason, that he might be revealed to Israel." JOHN 1:31

The Forerunner Prepares the Way

JOHN 1:19–34 ¹⁹*This is the testimony given by John when the Jews sent priests and Levites from Jerusalem to ask him, "Who are you?"* ²⁰*He confessed and did not deny it, but confessed, "I am not the Messiah."* ²¹*And they asked him, "What then? Are you Elijah?" He said, "I am not." "Are you the prophet?" He answered, "No."* ²²*Then they said to him, "Who are you? Let us have an answer for those who sent us. What do you say about yourself?"* ²³*He said,*

"I am the voice of one crying out in the wilderness,
'Make straight the way of the Lord,'" as the prophet Isaiah said.

²⁴*Now they had been sent from the Pharisees.* ²⁵*They asked him, "Why then are you baptizing if you are neither the Messiah, nor Elijah, nor the prophet?"* ²⁶*John answered them, "I baptize with water. Among you stands one whom you do not know,* ²⁷*the one who is coming after me; I am not worthy to untie the thong of his sandal."* ²⁸*This took place in Bethany across the Jordan where John was baptizing.*

²⁹*The next day he saw Jesus coming toward him and declared, "Here is the Lamb of God who takes away the sin of the world!* ³⁰*This is he of whom I said, 'After me comes a man who ranks ahead of me because he was before me.'* ³¹*I myself did not know him; but I came baptizing with water for this reason, that he*

might be revealed to Israel." ³²And John testified, "I saw the Spirit descending from heaven like a dove, and it remained on him. ³³I myself did not know him, but the one who sent me to baptize with water said to me, 'He on whom you see the Spirit descend and remain is the one who baptizes with the Holy Spirit.' ³⁴And I myself have seen and have testified that this is the Son of God."

John was a person of self-effacing honesty, who knew that his function was a preparatory one. He was sent from God "as a witness to testify to the light" (John 1:7). He says of Jesus, "After me comes a man who ranks ahead of me because he was before me" (verse 30). In this enigmatic phrase, the gospel alludes to the relationship between John and Jesus. Even though Jesus followed after the ministry of John, Jesus is the superior because he existed before John. The phrase points to the divine preexistence of Jesus and the priority of his saving work in God's plan. The role of John was to precede Jesus and to reveal him to the people of Israel.

As precursor of Jesus, John wanted to make sure that his role was not mistaken for that of Jesus. John stated that he was not the Messiah; he was not Elijah; and he was not "the prophet," the one like Moses anticipated for the messianic age (Deut 18:15). In response to the interrogators' question, "Who are you?" John replied with the words of Isaiah. He said he was the one crying out in the wilderness, telling people to prepare for the Lord's coming. John said that he was not even worthy to take off the sandals of the Coming One. Removing the sandals of the master was the task of the slave in the household. Everything that John said about himself prepared for his testimony about Jesus.

The important question of the gospel is not who is John, but who is Jesus. The voice in the wilderness is the first believer in the gospel. He accepted Jesus and then became his witness to others. John called Jesus "the Lamb of God" (verse 29), "the one who baptizes with the Holy Spirit" (verse 33), and "the Son of God" (verse 34).

As John, who urged Israel to prepare, was the messenger of Christ's first appearing, so John is the messenger today of Christ's reappearing in glory. Still he cries to the people of the twenty-first century: Prepare.

Reflection and discussion

- How does John demonstrate knowledge of his own strengths as well as his limitations?

  He knows what his job is doesn't overstep

- I, too, am called to witness to Jesus Christ. What is the content of my testimony?

  my life - how I live my commitment to God

- What does John the Baptist teach me about effective witnessing?

  allowing God to use him & not claiming power or importance that belongs only to God

Prayer

Coming One, though I am unworthy, you have called me to be a witness to you. Give me the insight to know who I am in God's plan and the courage to witness to your coming in my everyday world.

SUGGESTIONS FOR FACILITATORS, GROUP SESSION 3

1. Welcome group members and ask if there are any announcements anyone would like to make.

2. You may want to light a candle and pray this prayer as a group:
   Son of the Most High, ancient Israel awaited the dawn of your coming. Mary and Elizabeth, Zechariah and John the Baptist prepared the way for you. Stir up my heart and move me to genuine repentance so that I may make my life ready for your coming. Help us encourage one another as we wait for you, and give us joyful hope. Make us people of your word, trusting that what has been promised us will come to fulfillment.

3. Ask one or more of the following questions:
   - What new insight into the meaning of Advent did you gain this week?
   - What encouragement do you need to continue on the path of Bible reading?

4. Discuss lessons 7 through 12. Choose one or more of the questions for reflection and discussion from each lesson to talk over as a group. You may want to ask group members which question was most challenging or helpful to them as you review each lesson.

5. Keep the discussion moving, but don't rush it in order to complete more questions. Allow time for the questions that provoke the most discussion.

6. After talking about each lesson, instruct group members to complete lessons 13 through 18 on their own during the six days before the next group meeting. They should write out their own answers to the questions as preparation for next week's discussion.

7. Ask the group if anyone is having any particular problems with his or her Bible study during the week. You may want to share advice and encouragement within the group.

8. Conclude by praying aloud together the prayer starter at the end of one of the lessons discussed. You may add to the prayer based on the sharing that has occurred in the group.

**The days are surely coming, says the Lord,
when I will fulfill the promise I made.** JER 33:14

Fulfilling the
Ancient Covenant

covenant

JEREMIAH 31:31–34 *³¹The days are surely coming, says the Lord, when I will make a new covenant with the house of Israel and the house of Judah. ³²It will not be like the covenant that I made with their ancestors when I took them by the hand to bring them out of the land of Egypt—a covenant that they broke, though I was their husband, says the Lord. ³³But this is the covenant that I will make with the house of Israel after those days, says the Lord: I will put my law within them, and I will write it on their hearts; and I will be their God, and they shall be my people. ³⁴No longer shall they teach one another, or say to each other, "Know the Lord," for they shall all know me, from the least of them to the greatest, says the Lord; for I will forgive their iniquity, and remember their sin no more.*

JEREMIAH 33:14–22 *¹⁴The days are surely coming, says the Lord, when I will fulfill the promise I made to the house of Israel and the house of Judah. ¹⁵In those days and at that time I will cause a righteous Branch to spring up for David; and he shall execute justice and righteousness in the land. ¹⁶In those days Judah will be saved and Jerusalem will live in safety. And this is the name by which it will be called: "The Lord is our righteousness."*

 ^{17}*For thus says the Lord: David shall never lack a man to sit on the throne of the house of Israel,* ^{18}*and the levitical priests shall never lack a man in my presence to offer burnt offerings, to make grain offerings, and to make sacrifices for all time.*

 ^{19}*The word of the Lord came to Jeremiah:* ^{20}*Thus says the Lord: If any of you could break my covenant with the day and my covenant with the night, so that day and night would not come at their appointed time,* ^{21}*only then could my covenant with my servant David be broken, so that he would not have a son to reign on his throne, and my covenant with my ministers the Levites.* ^{22}*Just as the host of heaven cannot be numbered and the sands of the sea cannot be measured, so I will increase the offspring of my servant David, and the Levites who minister to me.*

a God who wants to be close

To the people of God who were living in exile in the land of Babylon, Jeremiah delivered a message of consolation and hope. But the change that would alter the fate of God's people did not consist of something absolutely new. It was, in fact, rooted in something very old—the covenant with God. The newness of the covenant signaled a new immediacy for that ancient relationship begun in Abraham, ratified through Moses, and transformed with David. The bond between God and his people would be forged in a new way. An integral part of the covenant, the Torah of God, would be written on people's hearts, so that it would be immediately personal and near (31:33).

Despite Israel's history of breaking the covenant through idolatry and injustice, God never abandons his people. God's promises are eternal. The covenant was made to last forever. Because God is steady despite people's failures, God can renew and transform the covenant. God says, "I will forgive their iniquity and remember their sin no more" (31:34).

This new covenant of God dawned in Jesus. He is the fullest expression of this covenant bond between God and his people. God kept his covenant made with Abraham by giving blessings to all the earth. God kept his covenant made with Moses by writing his law on people's hearts. God kept his promise made to David by giving an eternal throne to Jesus. With the coming of Jesus, all people "from the least of them to the greatest" (31:34) are destined to know God because of this most personal and intimate way in which God has come to us.

The promises of God's covenant remain as reliable as God's promises of the succession of the day and the night (33:20; see Gen 8:22). God's promises are as secure as the universe and as unalterable as time itself. Yet the fulfillment of prophecy is not something that happens one day and is then finished. Prophecy is not like yesterday's weather forecast that we can proclaim has either happened or not. God's promises are not over and done with when they are fulfilled; rather their fulfillment has a permanent and ongoing character.

God's ancient people knew that the focus of God's promise for the future involved the ancient line of King David. Jeremiah reiterated the prophecy of Nathan in 2 Samuel 7 that God would "cause a righteous Branch to spring up for David" (33:15). That Branch from the roots of Jesse (Isa 11:1) would rule with integrity and bring justice. In addition to an everlasting kingship (33:17), Jeremiah's prophecy assured God's people of an everlasting priesthood to offer sacrifices for all times (33:18). This double expectation of an eternal kingship and eternal priesthood led at least one Jewish group, the Essenes of Qumran, to expect both a kingly and a priestly Messiah. But the fullness of Jeremiah's words came with the eternal kingdom and priesthood of Jesus, whose reign and perfect sacrifice are established forever.

Reflection and discussion

- How has the new covenant both completed and transcended the original covenant?

- How does the new covenant enable us to "know the Lord" (31:34)?

*more we know J,
more deeply we know God
more faithful we are
more faithful God is*

- What two institutions of ancient Israel does God promise to re-establish? How does Christ fulfill this promise?

  everlasting priesthood
  everlasting kingship

- Israel seemed to need continual reminders and reassurance of God's covenant faithfulness. Why? Do I need the same?

  human
  sinful
  weak
  forgetful

- How faithfully has God fulfilled promises to me in the past? Am I secure in God's promises to me for the future?

Prayer

God of the covenant, you keep your ancient promises and never withdraw from me, despite my sin and withdrawal from you. Accept my repentance and create a new heart within me. Comfort me with your assurances and give me hope for the future.

The ox knows its owner, and the donkey its master's crib.

ISAIAH 1:3

Child in the Animals' Manger

ISAIAH 1:2–4, 16–20

²Hear, O heavens, and listen, O earth;
  for the Lord has spoken:
I reared children and brought them up,
  but they have rebelled against me.
³The ox knows its owner,
  and the donkey its master's crib;
but Israel does not know,
  my people do not understand.

⁴Ah, sinful nation,
  people laden with iniquity,
offspring who do evil,
  children who deal corruptly,
who have forsaken the Lord,
  who have despised the Holy One of Israel,
  who are utterly estranged!

[16]*Wash yourselves; make yourselves clean;*
    remove the evil of your doings
    from before my eyes;
cease to do evil,
    [17]*learn to do good;*
seek justice,
    rescue the oppressed,
defend the orphan,
    plead for the widow.

[18]*Come now, let us argue it out,*
    says the Lord:
though your sins are like scarlet,
    they shall be like snow;
though they are red like crimson,
    they shall become like wool.
[19]*If you are willing and obedient,*
    you shall eat the good of the land;
[20]*but if you refuse and rebel,*
    you shall be devoured by the sword;
    for the mouth of the Lord has spoken.

Ever wonder why the ox and the donkey are a compulsory part of every nativity display? The earliest images of the nativity present only three creatures: the baby in a manger, the ox, and the donkey. The many other characters were gradually added after this essential image was established in Christian tradition. The two animals are essentially symbolic; no one knows what animals may have been historically present at the birth of Jesus, for no animals are mentioned in the gospels.

Their presence in our nativity sets come from the opening image of Isaiah, a prophecy which is world shaking in its global significance: "Hear, O heavens, and listen, O earth" (verse 2). This is a proclamation for the whole universe. Even though God has lavished his care upon his people just as a parent cares for a child, they have rebelled against him. God's people have failed to understand what should be so obvious. In contrast, the prophet presents the image of the ox and the donkey, two animals notorious for their denseness and stubbornness, yet who naturally and instinctively recognize their owner (verse 3).

The image of the two animals at the manger or feeding trough indicates that they know the source of their life and ongoing welfare. With this image, the birth of Christ is presented in the context of salvation history. The coming of the Savior is God's response to a people who have turned away from their Master who feeds them. The universal context of the prophecy indicates that all peoples are destined to find the source of their life in the coming of the Messiah to Israel.

Isaiah proclaims that God's choice of the people of Judah implies for them both a blessing and a responsibility. God calls his people in increasingly intimate terms: nation, people, offspring, and children (verse 4). They have rejected God and failed to trust in him. God will not accept worship from those who deal corruptly and oppress the poor. Yet, forgiveness and healing are possible for the people of Judah if they learn to do good, seek justice, rescue the oppressed, and defend the helpless (verse 17).

The blessings and responsibilities of being God's children should be so obvious. The one kicking his feet innocently in a feeding trough shows us the way. Since the ox and the donkey recognize their master so instinctively, shouldn't we recognize the child in the manger as the source of our life and salvation?

Reflection and discussion

- If my response to God would be compared to that of an animal, what animal would it be? What do creatures of the animal world know that I sometimes forget?

- Which figures of the nativity scene teach me the most about the significance of Christ's coming?

- What does God call his people to do in order to experience forgiveness and healing (verses 16–17)?

change
confession
adult confessions
identify what blocks
root cause
ask for Grace - work at it

- In what ways might God be calling me to "seek justice" and "rescue the oppressed"?

Prayer

Lord of the Jews and Gentiles, you are the source of my sustenance and I depend upon you for my life. Help me recognize the obvious and appreciate the gifts you have given me.

**Those who lived in a land of deep darkness
—on them light has shined.** ISA 9:2

Light Shining in Darkness

ISAIAH 9:1–7 ¹*But there will be no gloom for those who were in anguish. In the former time he brought into contempt the land of Zebulun and the land of Naphtali, but in the latter time he will make glorious the way of the sea, the land beyond the Jordan, Galilee of the nations.*

²*The people who walked in darkness
    have seen a great light;
those who lived in a land of deep darkness—
    on them light has shined.*
³*You have multiplied the nation,
    you have increased its joy;
they rejoice before you
    as with joy at the harvest,
    as people exult when dividing plunder.*
⁴*For the yoke of their burden,
    and the bar across their shoulders,
    the rod of their oppressor,
    you have broken as on the day of Midian.*
⁵*For all the boots of the tramping warriors
    and all the garments rolled in blood
    shall be burned as fuel for the fire.*

⁶*For a child has been born for us,*
   a son given to us;
authority rests upon his shoulders;
   and he is named
Wonderful Counselor, Mighty God,
   Everlasting Father, Prince of Peace.
⁷*His authority shall grow continually,*
   and there shall be endless peace
for the throne of David and his kingdom.
   He will establish and uphold it
with justice and with righteousness
   from this time onward and forevermore.
The zeal of the Lord of hosts will do this.

Isaiah wrote at a time of great darkness for Israel, a time in which the land was being conquered and destroyed by the Assyrians. But in the midst of such desperation, today's verses shine out with brilliant hope. The prophet proclaimed that God would rescue his people from their subjugation—from the yoke, the bar, and the rod of their oppressors (verse 4). This deliverance was described as a burst of new light (verse 2) and new joy (verse 3) upon the darkness and gloom of the land.

This light and joy would be brought to the people through the birth of a child who would be king. This royal child was given titles that seem almost divine. The "Wonderful Counselor" designates one who devises wise plans and is able to carry them out. "Mighty God" designates a king who shares in the power of God to do whatever is necessary for the salvation of his people. "Everlasting Father" stresses his faithful, devoted care for his people. "Prince of Peace" expresses the peacemaking qualities of the king who would bring completeness and harmony to the kingdom under his reign.

God does not forget his promises, nor does God abandon his people in times of despair. Partial fulfillment of the prophecy was experienced in the lifetime of Isaiah, through successful battles and through kings who brought religious reforms, but the wondrous period about which the prophet foretold did not come about. Since the kings of the line of David were all considered

God's anointed and adopted sons of God, the people held high hopes for the reign of each new king. An ideal of kingship based on the best of the reign of David and Solomon and on Israel's understanding of divine kingship gradually developed. With the advent of each new king, the people's hopes flamed anew.

The followers of Isaiah projected his expectations into a more distant future, into the age of the anticipated Messiah. This Davidic king would be king and savior *par excellence*. In the Coming One, the kingdom of David would be characterized by justice, righteousness, and peace forevermore (verse 7).

Reflection and discussion

- How have I experienced God's deliverance from a heavy yoke? What present yoke do I desire God to break and shatter?

- Which of the Messianic titles (verse 6) best express my understanding of Christ?

Everlasting Father
faithful devoted
care for his people

Prayer

Wonderful Counselor, fill my darkness with the light of your wisdom and hope. Prince of Peace, banish the gloom of hatred and strife and bring the justice of your reign upon the earth.

He is the image of the invisible God, the firstborn of all creation. COL 1:15

Manifesting God to the World

COLOSSIANS 1:9–20 ⁹*For this reason, since the day we heard it, we have not ceased praying for you and asking that you may be filled with the knowledge of God's will in all spiritual wisdom and understanding,* ¹⁰*so that you may lead lives worthy of the Lord, fully pleasing to him, as you bear fruit in every good work and as you grow in the knowledge of God.* ¹¹*May you be made strong with all the strength that comes from his glorious power, and may you be prepared to endure everything with patience, while joyfully* ¹²*giving thanks to the Father, who has enabled you to share in the inheritance of the saints in the light.* ¹³*He has rescued us from the power of darkness and transferred us into the kingdom of his beloved Son,* ¹⁴*in whom we have redemption, the forgiveness of sins.*

¹⁵*He is the image of the invisible God, the firstborn of all creation;* ¹⁶*for in him all things in heaven and on earth were created, things visible and invisible, whether thrones or dominions or rulers or powers—all things have been created through him and for him.* ¹⁷*He himself is before all things, and in him all things hold together.* ¹⁸*He is the head of the body, the church; he is the beginning, the first-born from the dead, so that he might come to have first place in everything.* ¹⁹*For in him all the fullness of God was pleased to dwell,* ²⁰*and through him God was pleased to reconcile to himself all things, whether on earth or in heaven, by making peace through the blood of his cross.*

If Jesus Christ is the "image" of God (verse 15), then Christ's coming is a manifestation of God to the world. This image of God is more than a mere resemblance or similarity. The Greek word for "image" is icon. It is an exact representation, what we would call a portrait or photograph. The invisible God of the universe is made visible and revealed for humanity to see in Jesus Christ. He is the projection of God on the canvas of our humanity.

This "image" of God takes us back to the account of God's creation in Genesis. There the author tells us that God created humankind "in his image, in the image of God" (Gen 1:27). Man and woman were created to be nothing less than the "icon" of God, but sin marred that image. In Jesus, we see not only who God is, but also who we were meant to be. The coming of Jesus is the manifestation of God and the manifestation of our full humanity.

Paul states in his letter that he has been praying for the Colossians. His prayer is a model for genuine and sincere prayer for others, not just a glib or superficial sentiment. He prays specifically for the particular challenges that face his readers and he asks that they be filled with the wisdom and understanding of God and of God's will (verse 9). He prays that the Colossians will have the strength that comes from God and the patience to endure their trials (verse 11). Finally he prays that they experience joy and gratitude for what God has done for them—rescuing them from darkness, where the powers of evil hold sway, and bringing them into the light, enjoyed by the angels and the saints (verses 12–13).

Following his prayer, Paul inserted a hymn from early Christian worship (verses 15–20). It declares that Christ is not only the full manifestation of God and humanity, but also the source of all creation at its beginning and goal of creation at its end—"All things have been created through him and for him" (verse 16). Christ is supreme over all things, those in heaven and on earth, things that are visible and invisible. Truly he is Lord of the universe.

Reflection and discussion

- In what way does the coming of Christ reveal my true humanity?

- Which parts of Paul's prayer teach me new ways to pray for others?

- Which part of this hymn to Christ (verse 15–20) offers me new wisdom or understanding?

- What powers sometimes seem to be more powerful than Christ? How does this hymn reassure me?

Prayer

Christ the Lord, I cannot comprehend the vastness of God, but your coming reveals God to me with greater clarity. As I try to understand you more fully, lead me to a greater understanding of my own humanity.

When the fullness of time had come, God sent his Son, born of a woman, born under the law. GAL 4:4

Adopted as God's Children

GALATIANS 4:1–7 ¹*My point is this: heirs, as long as they are minors, are no better than slaves, though they are the owners of all the property; ²but they remain under guardians and trustees until the date set by the father. ³So with us; while we were minors, we were enslaved to the elemental spirits of the world. ⁴But when the fullness of time had come, God sent his Son, born of a woman, born under the law, ⁵in order to redeem those who were under the law, so that we might receive adoption as children. ⁶And because you are children, God has sent the Spirit of his Son into our hearts, crying, "Abba! Father!" ⁷So you are no longer a slave but a child, and if a child then also an heir, through God.*

Paul describes the state of waiting for Christ's coming with an analogy. We are heirs to a great estate, but we are still minors and cannot enjoy the benefits of our inheritance "until the date set by the father." As minors we are under the care of guardians and trustees, in a condition no better than the slaves of the household (verses 1–2). We are enslaved to worldly powers—fear, doubt, fatalism, suffering, and emptiness—to those aspects of the human condition that constantly threaten our true condition as heirs to glory (verse 3).

During the seasons of Advent and Christmas, this passage can speak powerfully to the experience of many. While the sights and sounds of the season urge us to be joyful, many are burdened with depression, disappointment, and despair greater than at any other time of the year. Try as they might, many cannot celebrate to fit the mood of angelic choirs and wise men bearing gifts. Enslaved to worldly powers, they cannot experience the glorious inheritance offered.

The coming of Christ, as Paul describes it here, entails Christ's realistic solidarity with the bondage of our earthly state. In the fullness of time, he came "born of a woman, born under the law" (verse 4). Christ comes into the depths of the human condition and takes on that condition in order to change it. He comes to "redeem," to buy us out of slavery (verse 5). In Christ, slaves become adopted children. Rather than raising us up to God's level where there are no more problems, Christ comes into our condition to give us access to a Father who loves us as his children. As children of the Father, we can claim our inheritance and enjoy our full rights.

Just as God sent his Son into the world, God sent the Spirit of his Son into our hearts (verse 6). God's Son redeemed us so that we could become God's children, and the Spirit enables us to know ourselves as legitimate children. Through the Spirit we can cry out "Abba! Father!" with the confidence of children who know their Father cares for them and hears their cries (verse 6). The Spirit personalizes the experience and assures us of our new status: "no longer a slave but a child, and if a child then also an heir" (verse 7).

consoling comforting

Reflection and discussion

- What are the worldly powers to which I am enslaved during this season?

- In what realistic ways does Christ's coming change my condition of slavery?

- What are my legitimate rights as an adopted child of God? What is my inheritance?

- What new understanding of the Trinity is offered to me by this description of the personal work of the Father, Son, and Spirit?

Prayer

Abba, you have sent your Spirit into my heart so that I can cry out to you with trusting confidence. Help me to live as your child with the freedom and confidence you want to give to me.

We wait for the blessed hope and the manifestation of the glory of our great God and Savior, Jesus Christ. TITUS 2:13

Waiting in Joyful Hope

TITUS 2:11—3:7 ¹¹*For the grace of God has appeared, bringing salvation to all,* ¹²*training us to renounce impiety and worldly passions, and in the present age to live lives that are self-controlled, upright, and godly,* ¹³*while we wait for the blessed hope and the manifestation of the glory of our great God and Savior, Jesus Christ.* ¹⁴*He it is who gave himself for us that he might redeem us from all iniquity and purify for himself a people of his own who are zealous for good deeds.*

¹⁵*Declare these things; exhort and reprove with all authority. Let no one look down on you.*

3 ¹*Remind them to be subject to rulers and authorities, to be obedient, to be ready for every good work,* ²*to speak evil of no one, to avoid quarreling, to be gentle, and to show every courtesy to everyone.* ³*For we ourselves were once foolish, disobedient, led astray, slaves to various passions and pleasures, passing our days in malice and envy, despicable, hating one another.* ⁴*But when the goodness and loving kindness of God our Savior appeared,* ⁵*he saved us, not because of any works of righteousness that we had done, but according to his mercy, through the water of rebirth and renewal by the Holy Spirit.* ⁶*This Spirit he poured out on us richly through Jesus Christ our Savior,* ⁷*so that, having been justified by his grace, we might become heirs according to the hope of eternal life.*

When a majestic visitor is expected in the land, the people clean up the villages and decorate the realm, making everything fit for the arrival of the expected one. They get rid of the mess and they add elements that enhance the beauty. A Christian is one who is always getting ready for the coming of our God and Savior, Jesus Christ.

The future coming of Christ is the constant motivation for the new life taken on by a disciple. This new life has a negative aspect: getting rid of the mess; and it also has a positive aspect: adding things that enhance. We put away irreverence, passing desires, malice, envy, and hatred (2:12; 3:3), and we take on the qualities of prudence, justice, and reverence (2:12). The coming of Christ has great power over our lives: negatively, freeing us from injustice and vice, and positively, giving us zeal for doing good deeds (2:14). This negative and positive sidedness of the Christian life is presented often in Paul's writings: crucifying our old self and being raised to new life (Rom 6:5–14); works of the flesh and fruits of the Spirit (Gal 5:16–26); and stripping off the old self and clothing the new self (Col 3:8–14).

When Christ our majestic visitor arrives, he makes us heirs of his kingdom and gives us eternal life (3:7). This great gift is not something that we have earned or that we in any way deserve (3:5). It is bestowed upon us because of God's great love for us, through the rebirth of baptism and the renewal of the Holy Spirit. This gift of our Savior fills us not with proud self-satisfaction, but with humble gratitude.

We live this life of grace between the first advent and the final advent. God's grace came to us in Christ's first coming; God's glory will appear fully in Christ's final coming. In this between times, we wait in joyful hope.

Reflection and discussion

- What mess do I need to get rid of to prepare for Christ's arrival?

- What attitudes, virtues, and behaviors would most enhance my life for the coming of Christ?

- What indicates to others that I am waiting in joyful hope between the first and final advents?

- How do the truths expressed in Paul's summary of faith (3:4–7) promote humility and gratitude in me?

Prayer

My Savior, thank you for making me your heir. Thank you for the gift of salvation. Thank you for my rebirth in baptism and my renewal in the Spirit. Thank you for blessing me with hope.

SUGGESTIONS FOR FACILITATORS, GROUP SESSION 4

1. Welcome group members and ask if anyone has any questions, announcements, or requests.

2. You may want to light a candle and pray this prayer as a group:
   Saving God, the ancient covenant begun in Abraham, ratified through Moses, and transformed with David finds its fullest expression in Jesus Christ. He is the Dawning Light, the Righteous Branch, the Wonderful Counselor, the Prince of Peace, the Icon of the invisible God. Through Jesus you have freed us from slavery and made us your children, heirs of your kingdom, calling on you as our Father. Give us grace as we read your living word, so that we may live in hope between the first and the final advent, awaiting the glory to be revealed.

3. Ask one or more of the following questions:
   - What is the most difficult part of this study for you?
   - What did you learn about waiting and preparing this week?

4. Discuss lessons 13 through 18. Choose one or more of the questions for reflection and discussion from each lesson to discuss as a group. You may want to ask group members which question was most challenging or helpful to them as you review each lesson.

5. Keep the discussion moving, but allow time for the questions that provoke the most discussion. Encourage the group members to use "I" language in their responses.

6. After talking over each lesson, instruct group members to complete lessons 19 through 24 on their own during the six days before the next group meeting. They should write out their own answers to the questions as preparation for next week's session.

7. Conclude by praying aloud together the prayer at the end of one of the lessons discussed. You may choose to conclude the prayer by asking members to pray aloud any requests they may have.

"Mary will bear a son, and you are to name him Jesus." MATT 1: 21

Son of David and Son of God

MATTHEW 1:18–25 *¹⁸Now the birth of Jesus the Messiah took place in this way. When his mother Mary had been engaged to Joseph, but before they lived together, she was found to be with child from the Holy Spirit. ¹⁹Her husband Joseph, being a righteous man and unwilling to expose her to public disgrace, planned to dismiss her quietly. ²⁰But just when he had resolved to do this, an angel of the Lord appeared to him in a dream and said, "Joseph, son of David, do not be afraid to take Mary as your wife, for the child conceived in her is from the Holy Spirit. ²¹She will bear a son, and you are to name him Jesus, for he will save his people from their sins." ²²All this took place to fulfill what had been spoken by the Lord through the prophet: ²³"Look, the virgin shall conceive and bear a son, and they shall name him Emmanuel," which means, "God is with us." ²⁴When Joseph awoke from sleep, he did as the angel of the Lord commanded him; he took her as his wife, ²⁵but had no marital relations with her until she had borne a son; and he named him Jesus.*

The infancy narrative of Matthew's gospel explains that the coming Messiah would be both Son of David and Son of God. Through the lineage of Joseph and his legal paternity, Jesus is Son of David;

through the Holy Spirit and the virginal maternity of Mary, he is Son of God. The obedient responses of both Joseph and Mary to the divine will were necessary for the coming of the Savior. In the Lukan account, Mary is the primary human actor, whereas Matthew's account emphasizes the response of Joseph to God's saving action in the world.

In calling Joseph "son of David" (verse 20) the angel evoked the messianic prophecies of the future king from David's line. By bringing Mary into his home in marriage, assuming public responsibility for their child, and by giving a name to the child, Joseph became the legal and adoptive father of Jesus. Because his father was of the line of David, Jesus legitimately became a descendant of David's royal lineage. Through Joseph, Jesus was able to be proclaimed as the Son of David, the Messiah of Israel.

We have no words of Joseph in any part of the New Testament. Yet, we know that he was a "righteous man" (verse 19) and willing to actively respond to God's grace. His choices were agonizing. Mary and Joseph were "betrothed," a legally binding relationship for a year or more before a couple shares the same home. Joseph could only assume that Mary had committed adultery. The evidence spoke for itself. Yet, out of love for Mary, he chose to quietly divorce her, without public accusation, trial, punishment, and shame.

The revelation in his dream cut short one agonizing choice and presented him with another, the choice to cooperate with the incredible workings of God. His life and his future were now out of his hands. His choice to do "as the angel of the Lord commanded him" (verse 24) caught him up in the cosmic drama wherein heaven and earth met in the child of Mary's womb.

The conception of the child in Mary's womb was revealed to be "from the Holy Spirit" (verses 18, 20). In the Hebrew Scriptures, the spirit of God was linked with God's creating power, the words of the prophets, and God's recreation in the last days. The work of the Holy Spirit in the womb of Mary both continues and culminates God's work throughout salvation history.

The text of Isaiah quoted in the Emmanuel prophecy (verse 23) proclaims and fortifies the Christian community's belief in the messianic identity of Jesus and his wondrous conception through the Virgin Mary. The translation, "God is with us," forms an overarching scheme of Matthew's presentation of Jesus' life from conception to the last verse of the gospel. In Jesus, God is with us and he will be with us always (28:20).

Reflection and discussion

- Though Joseph was not the biological parent of Jesus, why do the gospels call Joseph the father of Jesus?

- Have I ever received a dream that indicated God's will or gave me direction for my life?

- What do the willing responses of Joseph teach me about Advent trust?

Prayer

Spirit of the Living God, you hovered over creation and inspired God's prophets. Fall afresh upon me and fill me with renewed life. Give me inspiration and power to follow the divine will.

"The young woman is with child and shall bear a son,
and shall name him Immanuel." ISA 7:14

God Is with Us

ISAIAH 7:10–17 ¹⁰*Again the Lord spoke to Ahaz, saying,* ¹¹*Ask a sign of the Lord your God; let it be deep as Sheol or high as heaven.* ¹²*But Ahaz said, I will not ask, and I will not put the Lord to the test.* ¹³*Then Isaiah said: "Hear then, O house of David! Is it too little for you to weary mortals, that you weary my God also?* ¹⁴*Therefore the Lord himself will give you a sign. Look, the young woman is with child and shall bear a son, and shall name him Immanuel.* ¹⁵*He shall eat curds and honey by the time he knows how to refuse the evil and choose the good.* ¹⁶*For before the child knows how to refuse the evil and choose the good, the land before whose two kings you are in dread will be deserted.* ¹⁷*The Lord will bring on you and on your people and on your ancestral house such days as have not come since the day that Ephraim departed from Judah—the king of Assyria."*

This prophecy of Isaiah was an oracle of hope given originally to the house of David in the eighth century before Christ. The Davidic dynasty was again in jeopardy because of the invading armies threatening King Ahaz. Isaiah prophesied of God's willingness to provide a sign of assurance, a sign guaranteeing God's continual faithfulness to David's line (verses 10–11). Despite the king's refusal to ask for a sign, God provided the sign of Immanuel (verse 12–14).

The prophecy spoke of the approaching birth of a king, one who would assure the continuance of David's dynasty after a period of devastation. His birth and reign would bring restoration to the land and would be a sign that God truly was with his people. This prophecy of a Davidic reign over God's restored people did not find satisfactory fulfillment in the generations immediately following King Ahaz. The high ideals of these Immanuel prophecies (Isa 7, 9, 11) became a messianic hope for a future age.

The mother of the future king is called "a young woman" in the Hebrew text, but the Greek text of the Old Testament, the version more familiar to the early Christians, calls the woman "the virgin." In the Hebrew Scriptures, Israel is often referred to as a young woman, and sometimes specifically as a virgin (see Amos 5:2). The later Jewish period saw in Isaiah's words a messianic prophecy and proposed that Virgin Israel would give birth to the Messiah. Matthew's use of the text (Matt 1:23) expresses the Christian faith in the messianic identity of Jesus and his birth from the virgin Mary. Mary represents virgin Israel, implying that God's people cannot bring forth the Messiah from their own human history, but only through the direct intervention of God.

The title Emmanuel (Immanuel is an alternate spelling) means "God-with-us." God's promise, "I will be with you," made throughout history to God's patriarchs, kings, and prophets, is forever being completed in the one called Emmanuel. In the birth of Jesus, God's promise became effective and is now being confirmed and fulfilled throughout the life and eternal reign of Christ.

The quotation of this prophecy by Matthew's gospel in the infancy narrative of Jesus stresses the continuity between God's working throughout the ancient biblical tradition and God's new work in the coming of the Messiah. This first of many fulfillment quotations found throughout Matthew's gospel underlines the connection, more than the split, between the Old Testament and the New. Fulfillment of a passage from the Hebrew Scriptures in the life of Jesus does not remove the significance of meaning from the Old Testament or imply the end of Israel's tradition. It demonstrates, rather, the oneness of God's saving plan for all people and his commitment to be with us always.

Reflection and discussion

- Do I ever ask God for signs? How much do I rely on God's signs and promises?

- In what challenging times have I recognized that God is always with me?

- What is the meaning and significance in God's plan that Mary was a virgin?

Prayer

Emmanuel, help me believe that you are with me in the best and worst of times. Renew my hope in your promises and give me the trust I need to live with confidence.

> O Bethlehem of Ephrathah, from you shall come forth for me
> one who is to rule in Israel. MIC 5:2

O Little Town of Bethlehem

nothing more than a carol?

MICAH 5:2–5

²But you, O Bethlehem of Ephrathah,
    who are one of the little clans of Judah,
from you shall come forth for me
    one who is to rule in Israel,
whose origin is from of old,
    from ancient days.
³Therefore he shall give them up until the time
    when she who is in labor has brought forth;
then the rest of his kindred shall return
    to the people of Israel.
⁴And he shall stand and feed his flock in the strength of the Lord,
    in the majesty of the name of the Lord his God.
And they shall live secure, for now he shall be great
    to the ends of the earth;
⁵and he shall be the one of peace.

A dispute among the crowds in the time of Jesus witnesses to the widely held expectation about the origins of the coming Messiah: "Has not the Scripture said that the Messiah is descended from David and comes from Bethlehem, the village where David lived?" (John 7:42). The infancy narrative of Matthew's gospel states that the chief priests and scribes of Jerusalem knew that the Messiah's birthplace was to be Bethlehem of Judea (Matt 2:4–5).

The prophet Micah was a contemporary of Isaiah. He, too, foretold that a future ruler would bring salvation from threatening enemies. Like Isaiah, he introduced the future king by speaking of the queen mother who would give birth to the royal child (verse 3). The reign of this great king would extend "to the ends of the earth" (verse 4) and his rule would be characterized by peace (verse 5). Micah stated that the ruler would have deep historical roots; his "origin is from of old, from ancient days" (verse 2). This hinted that his reign was founded on the ancient dynasty of David and the eternal Davidic covenant. Like David the shepherd king, the coming ruler would "feed his flock" and bring security to his people (verse 4).

Bethlehem became well-known in Israel's history because it was the home of Jesse, the father of King David, and the birthplace of that greatest of Israel's kings. The double designation, "Bethlehem of Ephrathah," distinguished the town from Bethlehem in Zebulon (Josh 19:15). Ephrathah is the name of the clan of people who lived in the area of Bethlehem. Jesse is described as "an Ephrathite of Bethlehem in Judah" (1 Sam 17:12). The prophecy that the coming messianic ruler would come from Bethlehem implied that he would be a new David, come to fulfill all the promises God made through King David of old.

Bethlehem was a tiny village six miles south of Jerusalem. It was almost unnoticed and forgotten alongside mighty Jerusalem. Micah calls Bethlehem "one of the little clans of Judah"; but Matthew amends the text and calls Bethlehem "by no means least among the rulers of Judah" (Matt 2:6). Throughout biblical history, God has done wondrous things with those people and places who are the smallest, the least likely, and the unexpected. For example, God chose Gideon to deliver the Israelites, even though Gideon was from the weakest clan and the youngest in his family (Judg 6:15). Likewise, Saul declared that he was from the least of Israel's tribes, and David was the youngest of his brothers. The announcement that the Messiah and Savior of the world is the baby lying in a manger in Bethlehem is the fullest expression of this biblical theme that in God's hands, little is much.

Reflection and discussion

- Visit the little town of Bethlehem in your imagination. Why would God root his promises in a place like Bethlehem?

- What good things have come to me in small packages?

- In 1 Corinthians 1:26–29, Paul describes God's choice of the foolish, weak, and lowly in the world. In what ways does this theme continue in God's choices today?

Prayer

God of the covenant, through your choice of David you made Bethlehem a focus of your ancient promises. As I sing of the town of Bethlehem and imaginatively visit this hamlet of shepherds, fill me with awe at the wondrous way you have come to visit your people.

There, ahead of them, went the star that they had seen at its rising, until it stopped over the place where the child was. MATT 2:9

A Star Rises from the East

MATTHEW 2:1–12 ¹*In the time of King Herod, after Jesus was born in Bethlehem of Judea, wise men from the East came to Jerusalem, ²asking, "Where is the child who has been born king of the Jews? For we observed his star at its rising, and have come to pay him homage." ³When King Herod heard this, he was frightened, and all Jerusalem with him; ⁴and calling together all the chief priests and scribes of the people, he inquired of them where the Messiah was to be born. ⁵They told him, "In Bethlehem of Judea; for so it has been written by the prophet:*

⁶*'And you, Bethlehem, in the land of Judah,*
    are by no means least among the rulers of Judah;
for from you shall come a ruler
    who is to shepherd my people Israel.'"

⁷*Then Herod secretly called for the wise men and learned from them the exact time when the star had appeared. ⁸Then he sent them to Bethlehem, saying, "Go and search diligently for the child; and when you have found him, bring me word so that I may also go and pay him homage." ⁹When they had heard the king, they set out; and there, ahead of them, went the star that they had seen at its rising, until it stopped over the place where the child was. ¹⁰When they saw that the star had stopped, they were overwhelmed with joy. ¹¹On entering the house, they saw the child with Mary his mother; and they knelt down and paid him homage. Then, opening their treasure chests, they offered him gifts of gold, frankincense, and*

myrrh. ¹²*And having been warned in a dream not to return to Herod, they left for their own country by another road.*

The widespread expectation among the Jewish people of the coming messianic ruler was a threat to King Herod. He had taken upon himself the title "King of the Jews" as well as assumed the prerogative of the son of David by rebuilding the temple. His reign was noted for its murderous cruelty and he was insanely distrustful of any perceived threats to his power. So when news reached him that a child had been born who was destined to be king, conflict was inevitable.

The "chief priests and scribes of the people" knew the ancient prophecies that the Messiah was to be born in Bethlehem (verses 4–5). The passage quoted from the prophet Micah emphasizes that although Bethlehem is small, the town's stature is now great because the Messiah has been born there (verse 6; Mic 5:2). The last line of the Old Testament quotation refers to the anointing of King David many centuries before: "You shall be shepherd of my people Israel, you who shall rule over Israel" (2 Sam 5:2).

The idea that a new star marked the birth of a new ruler was common in the days of antiquity. But the Hebrew Scriptures told of a star that would mark the coming of the messianic king. In the days of Moses, a seer from the East named Balaam blessed Israel's future by proclaiming a coming king who would be announced by a star: "A star shall come out of Jacob, and a scepter shall rise out of Israel" (Num 24:17).

The wise men (*magi* in Greek) from the East, avid scholars of spiritual mysteries, undertook an arduous journey to honor the infant of whom great things were prophesied. Whether these seekers were from Persia, Arabia, Babylon, or other places to the East, their significance lies in that they were Gentiles from distant nations. Later tradition embellished the biblical account by giving names and royal titles to these magi: Melchior, king of Persia; Gaspar, king of India; and Balthasar, king of Arabia.

The gospels sets up a dramatic contrast between the violent rejection of Christ by the Jewish leaders and his willing and joyful acceptance by the Gentile strangers. Before we reproach the first-century leaders of Jerusalem, we may contrast the enthusiasm and devotion of converts from outside our faith

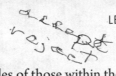

with the often indifferent attitudes of those within the church. We might also look within our own lives to contrast that part of ourselves that eagerly accepts the reign of Christ and the other part that persistently rejects his rule over us.

Reflection and discussion

- Why would the coming of the Messiah be threatening to some and evoke a violent response?

- Who are three wise seekers to whom I look for advice and guidance today?

- What can I learn about God from those outside my faith?

Prayer

Messiah of Israel, your coming was met with both acceptance and rejection. The message and deeds of your life on earth were received with both welcome and violent resistance. Help me open my heart to your presence and your word.

Nations shall come to your light,
and kings to the brightness of your dawn. ISA 60:3

Your Light Will Arise

ISAIAH 60:1–6

¹*Arise, shine; for your light has come,*
and the glory of the Lord has risen upon you.
²*For darkness shall cover the earth,*
and thick darkness the peoples;
but the Lord will arise upon you,
and his glory will appear over you.
³*Nations shall come to your light,*
and kings to the brightness of your dawn.

⁴*Lift up your eyes and look around;*
they all gather together, they come to you;
your sons shall come from far away,
and your daughters shall be carried on their nurses' arms.
⁵*Then you shall see and be radiant;*
your heart shall thrill and rejoice,
because the abundance of the sea shall be brought to you,
the wealth of the nations shall come to you.
⁶*A multitude of camels shall cover you,*
the young camels of Midian and Ephah;

> *all those from Sheba shall come.*
> *They shall bring gold and frankincense,*
> *and shall proclaim the praise of the Lord.*

This prophecy of Isaiah is a word of encouragement first spoken to the people of Jerusalem after their exile in Babylon. Their city was still in ruins and its social and religious structures devastated. The shining light is a metaphor for the glory of God to be manifested to his people (verse 1). Not only does Zion/Jerusalem receive God's light, but the city shines with the reflected light of God's radiance. The brightness cast on Zion contrasts with the darkness that covers the rest of the earth (verse 2). People and kings from many nations will come to Zion to see this dawning light, the glory of God revealed to Israel (verse 3). The joy that Israel's God brings to his own people shows forth his goodness and mercy to the whole world.

The image of light breaking forth in darkness is a majestic and timeless image that runs throughout Isaiah's prophecies, beginning with the splendid "The people who walked in darkness have seen a great light" (Isa 9:2) through God's promise, "I will turn the darkness before them into light" (Isa 42:16). In every age the image of light expresses God's saving entry into the murk of human bondage and suffering. The early church understood these ancient prophecies to point ultimately to Christ. The servant of God, called "a light to the nations" (Isa 42:6), is in due course shown to be the Savior of all the world.

Isaiah envisions a great procession to the holy city. First will come the dispersed sons and daughters of Israel (verse 4), who will be followed by people from many nations bringing gifts by camel caravans to proclaim the glory of God (verses 5–6). The mention of the retinue from Sheba is reminiscent of the visit of the Queen of Sheba to King Solomon (1 Kgs 10:2). From her distant land she visited the son of David, presenting him with gifts of gold, spices, and precious stones. Likewise, Psalm 72 sings of God's desire for David's son: "May the kings of Sheba and Seba bring gifts; May all kings fall down before him, all nations give him service" (Ps 72:10–11).

The adoration offered to Christ by the magi in Matthew's gospel represents the homage of all the nations to be offered the Messiah (Matt 2:11). Their gifts of gold, frankincense, and myrrh represent the tribute offered by the people of foreign lands in recognition of God's newly manifested presence in Israel. Even the well-known tradition that the magi traveled by camel is rooted in the words of the ancient prophets (verse 6). Both the prophets and the magi point to the universality of God's salvation offered in Christ.

Reflection and discussion

- Where on the scale from gloomy to radiant is my life in Christ? What would help me reflect his light more luminously?

- In what way does this text challenge me to be a global disciple and to extend my concern to all races and nations?

- What three gifts might I bring to honor Christ today?

Prayer

Lord of all nations, people throughout the world worship you and offer you homage. Though my gifts are simple, may they express my devotion to you and my desire to serve you with all that I have.

Out of Egypt I have called my son. MATT 2:15

Exiled Away from Home

MATTHEW 2:13–23 ¹³*Now after they had left, an angel of the Lord appeared to Joseph in a dream and said, "Get up, take the child and his mother, and flee to Egypt, and remain there until I tell you; for Herod is about to search for the child, to destroy him."* ¹⁴*Then Joseph got up, took the child and his mother by night, and went to Egypt,* ¹⁵*and remained there until the death of Herod. This was to fulfill what had been spoken by the Lord through the prophet, "Out of Egypt I have called my son."*

¹⁶*When Herod saw that he had been tricked by the wise men, he was infuriated, and he sent and killed all the children in and around Bethlehem who were two years old or under, according to the time that he had learned from the wise men.* ¹⁷*Then was fulfilled what had been spoken through the prophet Jeremiah:*

¹⁸*"A voice was heard in Ramah,*
wailing and loud lamentation,
Rachel weeping for her children;
she refused to be consoled, because they are no more."

¹⁹*When Herod died, an angel of the Lord suddenly appeared in a dream to Joseph in Egypt and said,* ²⁰*"Get up, take the child and his mother, and go to the land of Israel, for those who were seeking the child's life are dead."* ²¹*Then Joseph got up, took the child and his mother, and went to the land of Israel.* ²²*But when he heard that Archelaus was ruling over Judea in place of his father Herod, he was afraid to go there. And after being warned in a dream, he went away to the district*

of Galilee. ²³There he made his home in a town called Nazareth, so that what had been spoken through the prophets might be fulfilled, "He will be called a Nazorean."

Each of the four episodes in Matthew's second chapter is related to a place associated with a key feature of salvation history. Bethlehem harks back to God's choice of David (verses 1–12); Egypt recalls God's decision to free Israel from bondage (verses 13–15); Ramah is a reminder of Israel's captivity on Babylon (verses 16–18); Nazareth anticipates the life of Jesus (verses 19–23). Each episode also contains an Old Testament citation that contains the name of the place. In this way, Matthew demonstrates that the events surrounding the Messiah's advent happened in a way that "fulfilled" the Scriptures of Israel (verses 6, 15, 17, 23)—that is, in accord with God's plan. The quoted passages serve as a key to help the reader understand the events of Christ's coming more deeply by recalling the larger context of each passage as part of salvation history.

The quotation from Hosea 11:1, "Out of Egypt I have called my son" (verse 15), recalls the history of the Exodus while presenting the flight of Jesus' family to escape from Herod's wrath and their return from Egypt to Israel. The context of the passage from Hosea offers a tender, parental view of God for all those who wait in hope for God to act: "When Israel was a child I loved him…. I took them up in my arms…. I was to them like those who lift infants to their cheeks. I bent down to them and fed them" (Hos 11:1–4). This God who loves his people affectionately is the Father of Jesus, who cared for him in his infancy. The coming of the Messiah offers new hope for God's people, a hope rooted in Exodus and proclaimed by the prophets, that God will again redeem his people and lift them out of darkness.

Matthew's account of Jesus' infancy echoes the stories of Moses' birth and childhood. In both accounts there is a decree from a wicked king (Pharaoh and Herod) to slaughter the male babies (Exod 1:15–16), but the chosen child escapes in a wondrous way (Exod 2:1–10) while the other innocent infants are killed (Exod 1:22). In both accounts there is a flight to a foreign land to escape the king's decree (Exod 2:15) and then a divinely directed return to the land after the king's death (Exod 4:19). Beginning in the infancy account and continuing throughout the gospel, Matthew presents Jesus as a new and greater

Moses. As his great predecessor led the Israelites out of bondage, so Jesus will bring his people out of spiritual bondage and lead them to salvation.

As this infancy account points readers backward to Moses and the history of Israel, it also points them forward to the passion of Jesus. The suffering in these verses makes it clear from the beginning that Jesus would be rejected by many and that the redemption he offered would be accompanied by affliction and death. Already the shadow of the cross falls over the Christmas crib.

Reflection and discussion

- What are the places where God has led me as part of his saving plan?

- In what way do my parental instincts remind me of God's love?

- Why is it so essential for me as a Christian to know the Old Testament?

Prayer

Eternal God, you have shown your constant and faithful love in every age. Help me to place my hope in your steady care and know that your love for me will not leave me abandoned. Help me wait for you with trust and not with anxiety.

SUGGESTIONS FOR FACILITATORS, GROUP SESSION 5

1. Welcome group members and ask if anyone has any questions, announcements, or requests.

2. You may want to light a candle and pray this prayer as a group:
   Jesus, through angelic messengers and revelatory dreams, Mary and Joseph discerned their unique roles as instruments of your coming into the world. Through their obedient response to God's word, you were manifested as Son of David, Messiah, Emmanuel, dawning Light of the world, and King of all nations. Help us to receive God's word with faith and obedience, so that we might be instruments of your coming into the world today. Enlighten us as we gather in darkness to receive your light.

3. Ask one or more of the following questions:
   - What insight most inspired you from this week's study?
   - What new understanding of Advent did you learn this week?

4. Discuss lessons 19 through 24. Choose one or more of the questions for reflection and discussion from each lesson to talk over as a group.

5. Ask the group members to name one thing they have most appreciated about the way the group has worked during this Bible study. Ask group members to discuss any changes they might suggest in the way the group works in future studies.

6. Invite group members to complete lessons 25 through 30 on their own during the six days before the next meeting. They should write out their own answers to the questions as preparation for next week's session.

7. Ask the group how this study has affected the way they experience the seasons of Advent and Christmas this year.

8. Conclude by praying aloud together the prayer at the end of one of the lessons discussed. You may want to end the prayer by asking members to voice prayers of thanksgiving.

In those days a decree went out from Emperor Augustus that all the world should be registered. LUKE 2:1

Laid in a Manger

LUKE 2:1–7 ¹*In those days a decree went out from Emperor Augustus that all the world should be registered. ²This was the first registration and was taken while Quirinius was governor of Syria. ³All went to their own towns to be registered. ⁴Joseph also went from the town of Nazareth in Galilee to Judea, to the city of David called Bethlehem, because he was descended from the house and family of David. ⁵He went to be registered with Mary, to whom he was engaged and who was expecting a child. ⁶While they were there, the time came for her to deliver her child. ⁷And she gave birth to her firstborn son and wrapped him in bands of cloth, and laid him in a manger, because there was no place for them in the inn.*

Luke's account of the coming of Christ emphasizes its worldwide significance. Caesar Augustus was emperor of all of known humanity and was proclaimed as "savior of the whole world." He was acknowledged as divine and most recognized for the peace he established throughout the Roman Empire during his reign. Unknowingly he became an instrument of God's plan. His decree brought the parents of Jesus to Bethlehem for the birth of the true Savior, the one who brings real peace to the world.

The registration ordered by Augustus explains how Jesus, who was known to be from Nazareth, was born in Bethlehem in accordance with the messianic prophecies of the son of David. Because Joseph was from the family of David, he traveled with Mary from Nazareth to the village of his ancestors, Bethlehem of Judea (verse 3). The place of King David's origin became the birthplace of David's Son, Israel's Messiah.

While the entire world was on the move, an obscure couple made their way toward the small village of Bethlehem. With her child playfully kicking beneath her ribs, Mary quietly endured backaches and leg cramps during their long journey. The winter season of Palestine was unpredictable, at times blowing grit against their face and at times drenching them with rain. Reaching Bethlehem and searching for a place, they settle for a stable because the guest rooms were full. Mary's belly is a globe as round and full as the earth. The life inside her is about to become the life for the world.

The lowliness and simplicity of Jesus' birth is a strong contrast to the pageantry associated at the time with the imperial court in Rome. The Savior of all people entered history as a tiny, vulnerable creature. He was wrapped in bands of cloth, the traditional practice that kept a child warm and protected, and was laid in a manger (verse 7). The manger is a trough for feeding animals. He who will feed the whole world with the good news of salvation now lies in a manger because there was no place for him to lodge. Though the ox and donkey knew their master's manger (Isa 1:3), God's people would be slow to understand.

Throughout the life of Jesus, from beginning to end, he was exposed and vulnerable, from the cave of his birth to the cave of his burial. We see beyond Mary's holding Jesus in her arms as a baby to Michelangelo's Pietá with Mary holding Jesus across her lap once more, his head resting on her shoulder. The bands of cloth that wrapped his infant body become the linen cloth that wrapped his body for burial. The one who was laid in a manger would be laid in a rock-hewn tomb.

reality of the conditions
contrast
simplicity → royalty
pageantry

Reflection and discussion

- Do I recognize that all the world's peoples are cared for by God and share in my family life? Who are the people I tend to exclude from the family of God?

- How does the infancy account of Luke demonstrate that God works in ways that seem unlikely and unexpected?

- What mixture of feelings might have been welling up from the heart of Mary during these events?

Prayer

Savior of the world, you entered human history in a lowly place under simple circumstances. Expand my heart to include all the people loved by you and help me show signs of your love to everyone I meet.

Then an angel of the Lord stood before them, and the glory of the Lord shone around them, and they were terrified. LUKE 2:9

Savior, Messiah, and Lord

LUKE 2:8–20 ⁸*In that region there were shepherds living in the fields, keeping watch over their flock by night.* ⁹*Then an angel of the Lord stood before them, and the glory of the Lord shone around them, and they were terrified.* ¹⁰*But the angel said to them, "Do not be afraid; for see—I am bringing you good news of great joy for all the people:* ¹¹*to you is born this day in the city of David a Savior, who is the Messiah, the Lord.* ¹²*This will be a sign for you: you will find a child wrapped in bands of cloth and lying in a manger."* ¹³*And suddenly there was with the angel a multitude of the heavenly host, praising God and saying,*

¹⁴*"Glory to God in the highest heaven,*

and on earth peace among those whom he favors!"

¹⁵*When the angels had left them and gone into heaven, the shepherds said to one another, "Let us go now to Bethlehem and see this thing that has taken place, which the Lord has made known to us."* ¹⁶*So they went with haste and found Mary and Joseph, and the child lying in the manger.* ¹⁷*When they saw this, they made known what had been told them about this child;* ¹⁸*and all who heard it were amazed at what the shepherds told them.* ¹⁹*But Mary treasured all these words and pondered them in her heart.* ²⁰*The shepherds returned, glorifying and praising God for all they had heard and seen, as it had been told them.*

In Matthew, the Messiah's coming is manifested by a star to the magi; in Luke, the coming is manifested by an angel to the shepherds. The magi are wise men from the East; the shepherds are the lowly of the land, holding no social or religious status in Israel. Both magi and shepherds come to Bethlehem; they see the child and believe. They represent the people to whom the Lord's coming will be manifested throughout the gospels—the Gentiles from foreign nations and the lowly outcasts of the land of Israel.

The shepherds are the first to hear the gospel proclaimed, the "good news of great joy for all the people" (verse 10). That the good news was first announced to these simple people of the land set the tone for the entire gospel. Truly God has "lifted up the lowly" (1:52). Jesus would fulfill the words of Isaiah the prophet; he was the anointed one sent to bring good news to the lowly (Isa 61:1; Luke 4:18).

The angels' announcement is the message of the entire Gospel: the one born in Bethlehem is Savior, Messiah, and Lord (verse 11). As Savior, Jesus liberates people from sin and heals the divisions that separate people from God. As Messiah, Jesus is the anointed heir of David who will establish God's kingdom. As Lord, Jesus is the transcendent one invested with divine authority. The Jewish town of Bethlehem has become the focus of heaven and earth. The angels give glory to God who reigns in heaven and they evoke peace for the people of the earth (verse 14).

A baby wrapped in cloth and lying in a feeding trough is not the kind of "sign" (verse 12) one might expect at the birth of the Savior, Messiah, and Lord. The simplicity of the sign contrasts with the child's proclaimed identity. Both his poverty and his sovereignty invite us to ponder the mystery of this humble Savior who will call the lowly to himself. Because he did not choose wealth and power, we can come to him in rags and tags and unembarrassed. Because he became like us, we can become like him.

Reflection and discussion

- Of all the people of the world the angels could have visited, why would God want the Savior's birth first announced to shepherds?

- How might I want to imitate the response of the shepherds?

- What does the "sign" in Bethlehem teach me about my Savior?

- "Mary treasured all these words and pondered them in her heart" (verse 19). Why is Mary the model for Bible study?

  Do we ever treasure or ponder any God's words, Scripture passages?

Prayer

Savior, Messiah, and Lord, you were presented to the world in a lowly manger and announced to humble shepherds. I contemplate the mystery of your simple beginnings. Help me be a simple herald of this good news of great joy.

My eyes have seen your salvation,
which you have prepared in the presence of all peoples. LUKE 2:30–31

Light for Israel and the Gentiles

LUKE 2:22–40 ²²*When the time came for their purification according to the law of Moses, they brought him up to Jerusalem to present him to the Lord* ²³*(as it is written in the law of the Lord, "Every firstborn male shall be designated as holy to the Lord"),* ²⁴*and they offered a sacrifice according to what is stated in the law of the Lord, "a pair of turtledoves or two young pigeons."*

²⁵*Now there was a man in Jerusalem whose name was Simeon; this man was righteous and devout, looking forward to the consolation of Israel, and the Holy Spirit rested on him.* ²⁶*It had been revealed to him by the Holy Spirit that he would not see death before he had seen the Lord's Messiah.* ²⁷*Guided by the Spirit, Simeon came into the temple; and when the parents brought in the child Jesus, to do for him what was customary under the law,* ²⁸*Simeon took him in his arms and praised God, saying,*

²⁹*"Master, now you are dismissing your servant in peace,*
according to your word;
³⁰*for my eyes have seen your salvation,*
³¹*which you have prepared in the presence of all peoples,*
³²*a light for revelation to the Gentiles*
and for glory to your people Israel."

[33]And the child's father and mother were amazed at what was being said about him. [34]Then Simeon blessed them and said to his mother Mary, "This child is destined for the falling and the rising of many in Israel, and to be a sign that will be opposed [35]so that the inner thoughts of many will be revealed—and a sword will pierce your own soul too."

[36]There was also a prophet, Anna the daughter of Phanuel, of the tribe of Asher. She was of a great age, having lived with her husband seven years after her marriage, [37]then as a widow to the age of eighty-four. She never left the temple but worshiped there with fasting and prayer night and day. [38]At that moment she came, and began to praise God and to speak about the child to all who were looking for the redemption of Jerusalem.

[39]When they had finished everything required by the law of the Lord, they returned to Galilee, to their own town of Nazareth. [40]The child grew and became strong, filled with wisdom; and the favor of God was upon him.

The elderly man, Simeon, represents generations of devout Jews who longed with expectant faith for the coming of the Messiah (verse 25). God had assured Simeon that he would live long enough to see the Lord's Messiah (verse 26), and when this old man held the six-week-old Jesus in his arms, he recognized that the moment had come at last. Simeon could die in peace because in Jesus he had seen the salvation that God had prepared for all people (verse 28–32).

Simeon had studied the ancient prophecies to deepen his understanding of God's saving plan. As Mary and Joseph brought Jesus to the temple of Jerusalem to be presented to the Lord, Simeon recognized the child as the one sent by God to redeem both Israel and all the Gentile nations as well (verse 32). Within that place of ritual sacrifice, Simeon grasped something of the mysterious nature of Jesus' sacrificial life which would provoke opposition and bring suffering to the life of Mary and her Son (verses 34–35). Anyone who brings light also creates shadows. The "light of revelation" (verse 32) is a "sign that will be opposed" (verse 34). The sword that would pierce the heart of Mary (verse 35) reveals the shadow side of Jesus' saving work.

Anna the prophet also represents the people of Israel who had waited for the fulfillment of God's promises to send the Messiah and restore his people.

At the age of eighty-four, she lived in the Temple, fasting and praying, believing in hope that God would bring redemption (verses 36–38).

These two are Israel in miniature and Israel at its best: righteous, devout, at home in the temple courts, constant in prayer, led by the Spirit, longing and hoping for the fulfillment of God's promises. Both Simeon and Anna stood at the juncture where the old covenant met the new. Like Moses, who glimpsed at the Promised Land before his death, Simeon and Anna saw in the child Jesus what God had in store for his people. They remind us to heed the words of the psalmist: "Wait for the Lord; be strong and let your heart take courage; wait for the Lord!" (Ps 27:14). Yet they, like Zechariah and Elizabeth, are old and ready to move offstage. God is beginning something new, yet not entirely new, because hope is rooted in memory and God's new thing is the keeping of an old promise.

Reflection and discussion

- Have I grown impatient or complacent waiting for God's promises to be fulfilled in my life?

- What value have I found in waiting? What can Simeon and Anna teach me about waiting?

Prayer

Master Lord, my eyes have seen your salvation in the coming of Jesus. Teach me to wait in hope for the fulfillment of your promises at the end of my life and the end of the present world.

**The world came into being through him,
yet the world did not know him.** JOHN 1:10

True Light Coming into the World

JOHN 1:1–18 ¹*In the beginning was the Word, and the Word was with God, and the Word was God.* ²*He was in the beginning with God.* ³*All things came into being through him, and without him not one thing came into being. What has come into being* ⁴*in him was life, and the life was the light of all people.* ⁵*The light shines in the darkness, and the darkness did not overcome it.*

⁶*There was a man sent from God, whose name was John.* ⁷*He came as a witness to testify to the light, so that all might believe through him.* ⁸*He himself was not the light, but he came to testify to the light.* ⁹*The true light, which enlightens everyone, was coming into the world.*

¹⁰*He was in the world, and the world came into being through him; yet the world did not know him.* ¹¹*He came to what was his own, and his own people did not accept him.* ¹²*But to all who received him, who believed in his name, he gave power to become children of God,* ¹³*who were born, not of blood or of the will of the flesh or of the will of man, but of God.*

¹⁴*And the Word became flesh and lived among us, and we have seen his glory, the glory as of a father's only son, full of grace and truth.* ¹⁵*(John testified to him and cried out, "This was he of whom I said, 'He who comes after me ranks ahead*

of me because he was before me.'") [16]*From his fullness we have all received, grace upon grace.* [17]*The law indeed was given through Moses; grace and truth came through Jesus Christ.* [18]*No one has ever seen God. It is God the only Son, who is close to the Father's heart, who has made him known.*

The opening verses of John's gospel are just as much a Christmas story as the birth accounts of Matthew and Luke. In fact, this prologue of John's gospel has been the liturgical text for Christmas day since the early centuries of the church. Here there is neither angel nor manger, neither shepherds nor virgin mother. For John, the story of Jesus begins long before Bethlehem, in the realm of God's timeless eternity. There the Word existed with God and from there "the Word became flesh and lived among us" (verse 14). The coming of the Messiah is traced back not only through ancient Israel and God's prophetic promises, but, according to John, back to "the beginning" (verse 1).

Before the ages, "the Word was with God, and the Word was God." The Word, we might say, is God's self-expression, his reaching out, revealing the divine nature and sharing the divine life. The Word is distinct from God, but there is no separation between God and the Word. The first expression of God's word was creation itself. Throughout history, God spoke the divine word through the Torah and the prophets and wisdom. Finally this divine communication culminated in the fullest and ultimate Word, Jesus himself. The mission of Jesus, the Word, is to reveal to us the hidden nature of God, to show us by his life that God is loving, generous, caring, and forgiving.

Like the other biblical writers, John tells us that the coming of Christ into the world is something for which we must be prepared. At his historical coming, "the world did not know him" and "his own people did not accept him" (verses 10–11). But John intends his Gospel to help us receive him and believe in him, because through that faith we become children of God (verse 12). That is the ultimate reason why the Word became flesh: so that we might share intimately in God's life. As God's own children we are able to grow increasingly secure in our divine parent's love for us.

John refers to the Word as "the true light" (verse 9), "the light of all people" (verse 4). The motif of light and darkness is prevalent throughout John's gospel, describing the presence of Christ in the midst of earth's shadows and the darkness of sin, ignorance, and death. The glory of God is displayed for all to see in Jesus Christ, the light that shines triumphantly in a darkened world (verse 5).

Reflection and discussion

- Why did John choose to begin his gospel "in the beginning," rather than with the earthly conception and birth of Jesus?

- What is the best way to communicate love to another? Did God follow this way with us?

- Am I a person of my word? How are my words the extension of myself to others? Is God a person of his word?

Prayer

Son of the Most High, you responded to the waiting world with your remarkable condescension to assume human life. You became like me so that I could become like God. Help me to express my godlike nature to those I love.

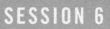
**We declare to you what we have seen and heard so that
you also may have fellowship with us.**

1 JOHN 1:3

Walking in the Light

1 JOHN 1:1–10 *¹We declare to you what was from the beginning, what we have heard, what we have seen with our eyes, what we have looked at and touched with our hands, concerning the word of life— ²this life was revealed, and we have seen it and testify to it, and declare to you the eternal life that was with the Father and was revealed to us— ³we declare to you what we have seen and heard so that you also may have fellowship with us; and truly our fellowship is with the Father and with his Son Jesus Christ. ⁴We are writing these things so that our joy may be complete.*

⁵This is the message we have heard from him and proclaim to you, that God is light and in him there is no darkness at all. ⁶If we say that we have fellowship with him while we are walking in darkness, we lie and do not do what is true; ⁷but if we walk in the light as he himself is in the light, we have fellowship with one another, and the blood of Jesus his Son cleanses us from all sin. ⁸If we say that we have no sin, we deceive ourselves, and the truth is not in us. ⁹If we confess our sins, he who is faithful and just will forgive us our sins and cleanse us from all unrighteousness. ¹⁰If we say that we have not sinned, we make him a liar, and his word is not in us.

are!
how trite we treat this!

The opening verses of John's first letter serve as both a prologue to the letter and a commentary on the opening verses of John's gospel. The focus of both the letter and the gospel is the Word—the Word that was "from the beginning" (verse 1). The gospel's climactic verse, "The Word became flesh and lived among us" (John 1:14), is amplified here with verbs of personal experience. The letter speaks of the Word that has been "heard," "seen," "looked at," and "touched." The truth about the identity of Christ cannot be separated from our earthly, bodily, sensual experience of him. Because God's Word was "revealed" to us, we can now "testify" and "declare" what we have experienced (verse 2).

John and the community he represents declare this message about the "word of life" so that those who hear it might have "fellowship" with them (verse 3). The goal of proclaiming the message is to bring people into communion, a union that is vertical as well as horizontal. This fellowship is with God and Christ as well as with the community of faith. This community is bonded with the Father and with the Son in a mutual indwelling that brings complete joy (verse 4).

"God is light" (verse 5). It is God's nature to reveal himself, to be fully authentic, to manifest divine love. And this God has done most fully in his Son, the light of the world. God is not only light in the abstract, but through Jesus the light has shown in such a way as to truly illumine human life. In human character and behavior there is always light and shadow, gray and shade. But God is completely light. This wonderful reality of God's Word made flesh forms the basis not only of our belief and proclamation, but also of our response in action. "Walking in the light" means that we think and live in God's sphere of being, that we live in ongoing fellowship with God and one another, and that we live as forgiven people (verses 7).

The work of Christ in the world is irrelevant to the human condition if he is not truly human. Apparently many within the community of John were unwilling to believe that "Jesus Christ has come in the flesh" (1 John 4:2). This first letter of John insists throughout on the fleshiness and the palpability of the Word in the world. The Word really became flesh and dwelt among us. The incarnation is real; the Son of God has come among us in the fullest possible way, in our humanity.

Reflection and discussion

- What difference does it make that God has revealed himself in the flesh? How do my five senses enhance my life in Christ?

- Does my belief in Christ draw me more deeply into Christian fellowship? Is this community a source of deep joy for me?

- In what way does the light of the world illumine the path in which I walk?

Prayer

Light of the world, you have come into our world so that we can see, hear, and feel your presence with us. Help me to walk in your light so that I may draw others to you and to the community of faith bonded in you.

"Surely I am coming soon."
Amen. Come, Lord Jesus!
REV 22:20

The Bright Morning Star

↙ last book in Bible
hard to read / understand

REVELATION 22:1–21 ¹*Then the angel showed me the river of the water of life, bright as crystal, flowing from the throne of God and of the Lamb* ²*through the middle of the street of the city. On either side of the river is the tree of life with its twelve kinds of fruit, producing its fruit each month; and the leaves of the tree are for the healing of the nations.* ³*Nothing accursed will be found there any more. But the throne of God and of the Lamb will be in it, and his servants will worship him;* ⁴*they will see his face, and his name will be on their foreheads.* ⁵*And there will be no more night; they need no light of lamp or sun, for the Lord God will be their light, and they will reign forever and ever.*

⁶*And he said to me, "These words are trustworthy and true, for the Lord, the God of the spirits of the prophets, has sent his angel to show his servants what must soon take place."*

⁷*"See, I am coming soon! Blessed is the one who keeps the words of the prophecy of this book."*

[8]*I, John, am the one who heard and saw these things. And when I heard and saw them, I fell down to worship at the feet of the angel who showed them to me;* [9]*but he said to me, "You must not do that! I am a fellow servant with you and your comrades the prophets, and with those who keep the words of this book. Worship God!"*

[10]*And he said to me, "Do not seal up the words of the prophecy of this book, for the time is near.* [11]*Let the evildoer still do evil, and the filthy still be filthy, and the righteous still do right, and the holy still be holy."*

[12]*"See, I am coming soon; my reward is with me, to repay according to every-one's work.* [13]*I am the Alpha and the Omega, the first and the last, the beginning and the end."*

[14]*Blessed are those who wash their robes, so that they will have the right to the tree of life and may enter the city by the gates.* [15]*Outside are the dogs and sorcerers and fornicators and murderers and idolaters, and everyone who loves and practices falsehood.*

[16]*"It is I, Jesus, who sent my angel to you with this testimony for the churches. I am the root and the descendant of David, the bright morning star."*

[17]*The Spirit and the bride say, "Come."*

And let everyone who hears say, "Come."

And let everyone who is thirsty come.

Let anyone who wishes take the water of life as a gift.

[18]*I warn everyone who hears the words of the prophecy of this book: if anyone adds to them, God will add to that person the plagues described in this book;* [19]*if anyone takes away from the words of the book of this prophecy, God will take away that person's share in the tree of life and in the holy city, which are described in this book.*

[20]*The one who testifies to these things says, "Surely I am coming soon."*

Amen. Come, Lord Jesus!

[21]*The grace of the Lord Jesus be with all the saints. Amen.*

The stance of watchful expectancy, the keynote of the Scriptures, comes to its peak in the Bible's last chapter. Three times the glorified Christ proclaims that the hopeful prayers of his people will be answered: "I am coming soon" (verses 7, 12, 20). The words are a prophecy of salvation history's climactic event which lies behind all the visions of Revelation. The book's final vision of the new heavens and new earth expresses humanity's trust that God will restore to all of creation what has been lost. Since Christ is "the Alpha and Omega, the first and the last, the beginning and the end" (verse 13), God's original plan for the world will be completed at the end. The long period of darkness over God's creation will be banished and replaced by the light of God's eternal dawn (verse 5) with Christ as its "bright morning star" (verse 16).

The Spirit, who was given by Christ to his church as its Advocate and Consoler, urges the church, Christ's Bride, to call on the Lord to "Come" (verse 17). The final prayer of the believing community, "Come, Lord Jesus!" (verse 20), is a translation of the ancient prayer from early Christian worship, "Marana–tha" (1 Cor 16:22). The prayer is found in the earliest known Eucharistic prayer, preserved in the Didache, and is a liturgical response that expresses the assembly's joyful yearning for Christ's coming, which the Eucharist celebrates and anticipates. Christ's promise that he is coming soon is the sum of all promises, and our prayer, "Come, Lord Jesus," is the sum of all hopes.

The author of Revelation is not concerned to calculate the timing of Christ's coming. Rather he intends to motivate his hearers to respond to Christ who is coming. He is not concerned with "when" but with "whom." Christ's coming is always at hand. The proper response of the Christian is to be watchful, to anticipate the Lord's coming with joyful hope. When we live in expectation, we will be ready for that great day when lamps and candles will no longer be necessary, when the glory of God will be our light. But until that glorious day, let's keep lighting candles to brighten up the darkness around us and to show us the path for our journey.

Reflection and discussion

- How does the Eucharist both celebrate and anticipate the coming of Christ?

- What do I need in order to entrust my future to God?

- What are my hopes for the coming new year?

Prayer

God who is the first and the last, the beginning and the end, increase my belief that you are faithful and true and deepen my trust that you hold the key to my future. As I face a new year, give me hope in your promises.

SUGGESTIONS FOR FACILITATORS, GROUP SESSION 6

1. Welcome group members and make any final announcements or requests.

2. You may want to light a candle and pray this prayer as a group:

   Son of God and Son of Mary, you were born into our world and laid in a manger. You came to live among us in our human flesh, in the humility and simplicity of a child. At your birth, heaven was joined to earth like fingers touching, as the angels sang and the shepherds drew near. We welcome you into our world again this Christmas, as we burn the holiday lights and candles in your honor. We believe that you are the eternal Word made flesh and dwelling among us, and we worship you as the Savior, Messiah, and Lord. Help us remember the reason for the season, and change our hearts to be like your own.

3. Ask one or more of the following questions:
   - In what way has this study challenged you the most?
   - What words do you think of now when you think about the season of Advent?

4. Discuss lessons 25 through 30. Choose one or more of the questions for reflection and discussion from each lesson to discuss as a group.

5. Ask the group if they would like to study another book in the Theshold Bible Study series. Discuss the topic and dates, and make a decision among those interested. Ask the group members to suggest people they would like to invite to participate in the next study series.

6. Ask the group to discuss the insights that stand out most from this study over the past six weeks and how the lights of Advent will hold a richer meaning from now on.

7. Conclude by praying aloud the following prayer or another of your own choosing:

   Holy Spirit, you cry out within us, the living Church, Come, Lord Jesus, Come. We believe that Christ will come in glory to finish what was begun at creation. We await with joyful hope the completion of God's reign, when the Lord will be our light and we will reign with him forever. Continue to deepen our love for the word of God in the holy Scriptures and draw us as disciples to receive the light of Christ. Bless us now and always with the fire of your love.

Ordering Additional Studies

AVAILABLE TITLES IN THIS SERIES INCLUDE...

TWENTY-THIRD
PUBLICATIONS

TO CHECK AVAILABILITY OR FOR A DESCRIPTION
OF EACH STUDY, VISIT OUR WEBSITE AT
www.ThresholdBibleStudy.com
OR CALL US AT **1-800-321-0411**